Separate Realities, Parallel Dimensions, Sorcerer's Apprentice, Season of the Witch

Psychic Warriors, MKULTRA, LSD

(a true story)

("What is truth? -- Pontius Pilate)

Rhawn Gabriel Joseph

Separate Realities, Parallel Dimensions, Sorcerer's Apprentice, Season of the Witch

Psychic Warriors, MKULTRA, LSD

Rhawn Joseph Gabriel

ISBN: 978-1-938024-35-1

Contents

1 The Separate Reality: A Sonora Day in Search
of a Sorcerer   4

2. Project ULTRA: Assassins, Psychic Warriors, LSD   23

3. Body Snatchers, Shape Shifters, Black Holes,
Eaters of Souls: The Sorcerer Speaks   39

4. Season of the Witch: The Demon Princess Queen   50

5. Warriors: Killing Devils and Demons   61

6. Owl Woman and the Warlock   77

7. The Door to Past Lives and Multiple Realities   88

8. Seeing vs Looking, Multiple Futures, Parallel
Dimensions, Magic is Technology   103

9. Passageways to Separate Realities. Transmigration
of Souls: To Die and Be Reborn   120

10: To See as Gods! A Door Opened - A Door Closed   131

1 The Separate Reality: A Sonora Day in Search of a Sorcerer

The desert Sonora sun was at 12 o'clock high and my head would have baked to a crispy brown if not for the denim cowboy hat which provided a semblance of shade for my sweating brow. I was cruising along highway 15, in a brand new 1969 rag-top VW Beetle, in search of a "Brujo" --a Yaqui Sorcerer known only to me by his alias: don Juan Matus.

I sped up, the odometer rapidly clocking away the desert miles. There wasn't much to see: Cactus, gullies, canyons, low mountains and an occasional dead animal broiling on the hot asphalt pavement. Perhaps every hour or so I would pass an ancient old woman or sometimes two wrinkled old crones dressed in black or the standard peasant-Indian garb, bundles balanced on their heads, walking slowly alongside the dusty road, going who knows where, as there were no houses or stores, and the nearest village was usually dozens of miles away.

I had begun my search just three weeks prior, in a little border town near the Arizona Sonora border; my luggage consisting of food, water, weed, guitar, Pentax camera, extra clothes, camping gear, several books including my personal copy and a Spanish-translation of a dog-eared paper-back book, "The Teachings of don Juan"; and, courtesy of General Wheeler and "The Company" about $3000 in cash, a Colt 45, and a Kodak Instamatic Movie Camera stowed in the trunk.

This was my second "assignment" for "The Company"--which, at first, I eagerly embraced. Escaping induction into the Army and death in the jungles of Vietnam was just icing on the cake. My "cover story" was to be "me."

What exactly "The Company" was, I didn't know, though I had my suspicions. But I did know General Wheeler, met him twice in 1966, when I was "dating" his granddaughter, Carrie, the first love of my life. The General lived in a colonnaded brick mansion on a military base in Virginia, his servants: captains and lieutenants who served lunch, and on another occasion dinner, as Wheeler questioned me about "California", "beatniks", "hippies", "LSD," "ESP," the "Berkeley Free Speech Movement" and the "war in Vietnam," and then listened thoughtfully to my replies.

At that time my family was living in a diplomatic community in McLean Virginia. It was not uncommon for the parents of my friends--generals, ambassadors, elected officials--to engage me in detailed discussions. My girlfriend, Carrie's father was probably CIA, and when he made one of his infrequent visits home, even he would talk to me. I was well read, articulate, and from sunny California which always piqued their interest.

Two years later, after moving back to the Golden State, I was assigned draft lottery number 52. Having taken a year off before starting college I was now facing certain induction into the Army's meat grinder war machine. Vietnam here I come! Hell no, I didn't want to go; but what was I to do? That's when Wheeler's emissaries made me an offer I would have been crazy to refuse.

Following three months of "training"--first by the military and then at a research center in Palo Alto-- I was now doing exactly what, initially, I would have loved to do: search out and locate a Yaqui Sorcerer, AKA: don Juan Matus.

After three weeks of fruitless searching, I was growing bored and nearly out of weed. I'd stopped at dozens of Mexican villages, towns, and open air markets, often more than once, approaching men and women I assumed to be Yaqui Indians, waving the "The Teachings of don Juan", and asking, in my rudimentary Spanish, as to the whereabout of this "Yaqui Brujo, Juan Matus." I had no luck at all. The Mexicans and Indians would glance at the book then at me, puzzled and uncomprehending; some making the sign of the cross as they hurried off or backing away as if I was mad and dangerously insane.

My last stop had been a dry, dusty little town with a crowded open air market. As usual, I'd been asking questions, getting nowhere.

Finally, I spied a clapboard medicine booth consisting of four wooden posts, cross beams, and an overhead tarp to block the sun. There were two wooden tables, and book shelves laden with a variety of dried plants, mummified animal parts and fluid filled jars with who knows what swirling inside. From a post hung a hand lettered cardboard sign which announced in Spanish: "Medicinal Plants." A grizzled old man, wearing a straw hat and white cotton shirt was strolling back and forth in front of this booth, a withered plant in one hand, a dead snake in the other, singing, in sing-song Spanish, that his medicines could cure any illness, the dreaded names of which he recited in beats of four thus giving rhythm to his cadence.

He and I glanced into the sky. A black crow, or maybe it was a raven, was circling overhead.

Book in hand, I approached the old medicine man, introduced myself, handed him the Spanish translation of "The Teachings," then stated my purpose: "I'm looking for don Juan Matus. He is a healer who is renowned for his knowledge of medicinal plants. Have you heard of him? Do you know where I can find him?"

The old man didn't seem to understand. Instead he led me to his booth and tried to sell me some of his concoctions.

I noticed then, sitting in shadows of his stall, a wrinkled old crone, gray haired and as old as the hills. She looked mummified. I wasn't sure if she was dead or alive.

Then, a flutter of wings, a slight breeze, and, as if out of nowhere, a green eyed beauty with long hair as black as night, stepped up to the booth and began inspecting the wares as she absently cooled herself with a dark feathered fan. She was dressed in a black tight fitting blouse and skirt, which emphasized her many charms. I studied her in profile. Wow. She was shockingly beautiful, a true "Foxy Lady." What a babe!

She glanced my way. Eyes of fire, face of desire, and lips like the sun. Smitten I gave her my most charming smile--but the old medicine seller stepped between us, holding up a clutch of herbs, trying to get my attention.

Again, I showed him "The Teachings of don Juan", and asked, in my rudimentary Spanish, as to the whereabout of this "Yaqui Brujo."

"Brujo! Brujo!" I repeated.

The ancient old crone in the shadows suddenly came to life; her eyes clouded with muck, staring blindly. She waved one hand in a circling motion, and mumbled under her breath. The old man, his face a worried frown, took several steps back away from me.

The beauty in black was glaring, her eyes narrowed, glowing, like a bird of prey. She cursed in Spanish, took a step toward me, and using her fan began shooing me away, forcing me to step back as I held up my hands and repeated stupidly: "Eres una mujer hermosa" and "Nina hermosa" (You are so beautiful!)

My attempts at charm and charisma were rewarded with mumbled curses. To my added surprise, she raised her hands and arms above her head, mumbling strange words and oaths. Even so, she was stunningly beautiful! A total foxy lady! Too bad she was nuts! What the hell was wrong with her? Then, her blazing eyes upon me, more curses.

Others were gathering and watching with interest as she spat and cursed and flicked her black feathered fan. The prospect of getting arrested and ending up in a Mexican jail for, who knows what, had no charms for me. I made my escape, found my car, and headed for the highway.

There was almost no traffic along this asphalt-smoldering two lane desert highway. The cactus-studded landscape was arid, hot, and boring. To the side of the road, only the occasional carcass of a cow, horse, dog, or the remnants of various creatures which, after having been smacked by some car, lay rotting and cooking in the desert sun.

I still had a quarter tank of gas, which is not much when driving in the heart of the Sonora desert with a broiling sun up above. I should have gassed up at that last village, but, in my haste to escape, gas had been an after thought.

Up ahead I could see a cluster of adobe hovels and shacks surrounded by a graveyard of wrecked disembodied cars, and old tires piled in heaps. I spied an ancient "Pemex" gas pump, and two old men on a wooden bench.

I glided to a stop beside the single, old fashioned, glass-caped gasoline pump, leaving clouds of dust in my wake. I glanced at the two old men who sat together in the shade of dozens of stacked tires, waiting, for what? A bus maybe? I reasoned.

I heard the flapping wings before I saw the bird, which made me think of the beautiful black-clad Yaqui woman who, that morning, had chased me off with a flicking of her feathered fan. There was no woman this time. Instead, a big black crow, the sun gleaming off its shiny wings, made a two-point landing on the hood of my VW. Its side-mounted eyes narrowing over its beak, it cocked its head to the left and right staring as I stared back.

The two old men stood up, shading their eyes as they peered into the distant sky. I followed their gaze and spied what I thought might be a small plane, but as it flew closer, descending toward the desert sands, I thought: Eagle? Condor? It was holding something in its talons.

A tall but skinny sun-browned Mexican man, the owner of this gas station, wiping his hands on a dirty rag, emerged from the nearest shack which had a small dust covered dilapidated sign reading "Cantina." A short, fat sweating woman and two dirty squirming brats stood in the ancient wooden doorway watching.

The crow with several flaps of its wings, took two steps across the hood of my car. My eyes followed. Had that eagle just landed back behind the "Cantina" Pemex gas station? No. Not likely.

And then, the crow flapped its wings, and was gone.

Stepping out of the car, I stretched, and thought about rolling a joint. But it was just too hot.

The owner and I quickly reached an agreement on the price of gas which he proceeded to pump into my tank. Fetching my Spanish edition of "The Teachings," I began peppering the owner with questions about "don Juan."

"No comprehende," he kept repeating, his eyes firmly on the nozzle, his focus entirely on pumping gas.

Fuckin A! I was bored, frustrated. This was no fun at all. Total bummer. Complete waste of time. What bad luck. If not for the new draft lottery, I would never have accepted this deal, and would probably be on a Santa Cruz beach with a beautiful babe soaking up the California sun. But I got lucky number 52; and within weeks a draft notice and orders to report to the Army Induction Center in Oakland.

Wheeler's men showed up next. The deal was simple: I could serve my country and the military, without serving in the military; and, would receive training in weapons, tactics, martial arts, $2,000 a month plus traveling money, and a guarantee I would never have to kill anyone or spy on my friends in the anti-war movement. The former but not the latter, turned out to be a damned lie. When I seemed doubtful, one of Wheeler's emissaries began talking about "James Bond" and said I would be "fucking a lot of hot chicks!"

"Fuckin A! Sign me up!"

James Bond? Another lie. Hot chicks? Well, there are always women looking for Mr Right Now. As to finding "don Juan," yeah, that did seem interesting, exciting at first. But now I was wondering if "don Juan" even existed and if Castaneda's book was total bull shit.

Fuckin' A! It was hot!

"Coca cola?" I asked the owner his eyes still on the nozzle. He nodded toward the open door of the "Cantina" just as an ancient old man, his back bent with age, his face a roadmap of wrinkles, strolled slowly from around the side of the building. He was barefoot, no hat, dressed in a very clean white-tanned cotton shirt and pants, and carried a large tethered brown leather sack about the size of a shopping bag in his left hand. He looked to be 100 years old!

The two old bench warmers leapt up at his approach, bowed with respect, and each kissed a ring on his right hand. I silently observed as they exchanged words and then money for tightly wrapped packages of varying size which the ancient old man retrieved from his leather sack.

The old man next spoke to the fat woman in the doorway and handed her a small parcel. She looked at me and nodded. Then the two of them stepped inside the Cantina. In less than a minute the old man, or his son, stepped outside.

I blinked my eyes. The sun must have broiled my brain!

What had been a wizened old man, bent with age, did not look ancient at all. The wrinkles were almost gone, his silver-grey hair nearly black; he exuded energy, charisma, vitality. I would have guessed him to be maybe 50. Yeah, he was still old, but certainly no Methuselah!

Sidling up, and giving the inside of my convertible VW admiring glances, the man introduced himself as "don Valencia Rojas" and asked if I would give him a ride.

He looked harmless, but I was wary. He could have a gun in that sack, and next thing I know, I'm not just giving him a ride, but my car and my life.

He seemed to read my thoughts, and with a laugh opened his sack and said: "See, I have no guns. No knives. Just me."

Well, I did receive six weeks of weapons and martial arts training, and another week where I'd been forced to put them to use; so, what the hell.

"Where are you going?" I asked.

"As far as you care to journey," he replied.

"What's that supposed mean?" I asked.

"Your car is pointed East."

"Sure, get in. First, though, I need to get a cold coke and talk to those men," I said, but then realized the two old men were gone.

Five minutes later, a Coca Cola in hand, we were on the road, the sun now aimed like a heat-seeking missile at the back of my broiling neck. There was no temptation to put the top up. With no air conditioning we would be baked alive. The wind was our air-conditioning.

"don Rojas" apparently didn't mind the heat. He was becoming so talkative I had to interrupt him to bring up "don Juan" and show him the book.

He laughed, his eyes sparkling with mirth as he gazed at "The Teachings," and said: "A paper back book! Careful, when in the deserts of Mexico, the peasants use those books for toilet paper."

Then he said, in a mixture of English and Spanish: "Maybe I can help you find what you are looking for."

"And what am I looking for?" I asked.

"Maybe a little smoke? Maybe mescalito?" He held out his brown leather sack, the mouth of which was secured by strings of leather. "Isn't that what all the young Gringos search for down here? Or maybe you desire a beautiful dark-eyed Senorita to keep you warm on cold desert nights."

Again I showed him the book. "I'm looking for a Bruja. A sorcerer. don Juan Matus. This book tells his story. I'm searching for him."

don Rojas began laughing and slapping his thigh between laughs.

"Why's that funny?" I asked, annoyed.

Between chuckles, he replied: "A Bruja is no sorcerer. A Bruja is an evil witch, a servant of Diablo. A Bruja will eat you. Only a brujo is a sorcerer. You Gringos. Always searching never finding, never seeing what is right before your eyes."

"What's that supposed to mean?" I asked.

don Rojas stopped laughing and gazed at me seriously: "Searching is looking without seeing. Without knowing. Seeing is knowing!" he said. Then he laughed.

I slowed the car to a crawl and met his gaze. His eyes were twinkling with mirth; as if he knew something I didn't; as if I was the butt of a secret joke and he found me immensely amusing.

"Seeing is knowing? Knowing is seeing?" I repeated. "That sounds like a tautology. Circular reasoning. Meant to sound heavy, deep, when its just words."

"A true sorcerer," he replied, "a Tetlachihuic can make magic with words."

"Tetlachihuic?" I asked.

"A magician. Tetlachihuics are true sorcerers, serving neither good nor evil but who can do both good and evil, even call upon a demon from hell, just by saying its name."

"And how do you know all this?" I asked.

don Rojas, laughing and slapping his thigh, simply said: "Maybe a little bird told me."

"A little bird?" I asked. "I don't understand what you're talking about."

"You are not seeing," he replied. "Not really. Not yet."

I put the car into third gear and speeded up.

"Explain!" I demanded.

"You and I saw each other before I asked for a ride," he answered.

"Yes, of course," I replied. "You walked around the corner of the building first. Then we met."

"No no. Before that!" don Rojas insisted. He was no longer laughing. He seemed disappointed.

"You mean in one of the villages?"

"No. Think," he said. "You came here hoping to learn to see. So see. If you do not wish to see, then go home and be blind. Continue to sleep, to never awaken to the layers of reality of which this world is only a fragment."

"Some people believe life is but a dream," I replied.

"Is that so?" He asked. "Then, maybe, I am dreaming you."

"Or vice versa," I answered.

"Or maybe god is dreaming us both," he replied.

"Have you been to college?" I asked. "You seem well educated."

"The world is my university," he answered. "I have read many books of knowledge."

I put the car in fourth gear, accelerated and pondered his comments and the possibilities.

"Are you a Brujo?" I asked.

He frowned at me. "Some say I am a doctor. Médico."

"What kind of doctor? What's your speciality?"

don Rojas ignored my questions.

"You say we met before. I think you're mistaken," I said, giving him a sidelong glance.

"Not met. Seen! Visto!" he answered. "I was expecting you."

Expecting? My thoughts began to race. Feeling uncomfortable I slowed the car to a crawl, stared at him, searching his smiling face.

"Why were you expecting me? What do you mean by that? And where did we see each other? When did this happen?" I demanded.

"Today," he answered. "This afternoon. You were seeing. Think! Try to remember!"

I thought hard. Then sniggered a laugh, convinced he was talking bull shit, trying to make a fool out of me.

"A crow landed on the hood of my car at the gas station. Are you trying to tell me that was you?"

don Rojas began laughing uproariously and slapping his thigh between laughs. "Don't be ridiculous. Of course not."

I pulled to the side of the road, careful not to stray too far for fear the tires might sink in the sand.

"Is this where I get out?" he asked.

"I also saw an eagle," I said in a challenging voice.

"So you did see," he replied thoughtfully.

Was he claiming to be an eagle? Not for a moment did I believe him. I began laughing. But don Rojas didn't laugh. He was staring with such intensity it felt as if two hands had taken hold of my head and were squeezing the thoughts right out of my brain. I didn't like it at all. I began to feel anxious, maybe a little afraid.

I kept the car in neutral, undecided if I should kick him out, which seemed like the smart thing to do. That's when he put his hand inside the leather bag sitting on his lap, which made me wonder if it contained a hidden weapon.

"What's in the bag?" I asked, trying to be nonchalant as I positioned myself into a defensive posture.

"Magico," he replied. don Rojas pulled out a writhing, hissing green serpent which he waved in front of my face. It's forked tongue licked the air to determine if I might be something good to eat.

"Fuckin' A. Is that thing poisonous?"

"You are looking, but not seeing," he answered.

The serpent became a squawking green parrot which looked at me wild-eyed. Then the parrot became a green handkerchief embroidered with serpents and parrots which don Rojas used to wipe the perspiration from his face, then blow his nose.

I was stunned. This was no cheap magic trick. Or was it?

"Are you a wizard? A sorcerer?" I asked.

"I've been called worse," he answered with a self-depreciating shrug. "Are we going to drive or just sit here in the hot sun."

I put the VW back in gear and we continued down the broiling, desolate, desert highway.

"Are you don Juan? The don Juan in this book?" I asked excitedly.

"A real sorcerer, a true magician would never tell anyone his true name," don Rojas answered.

"Why's that?"

"Power. Those who know the true names of the demons, diablos, sorcerers and creatures which haunt the cosmos, can call upon them, and use their power for good, or evil."

"Creatures of the cosmos?" I asked.

don Rojas gave me a look of disappointment: "Certainly, my young gringo amigo, you did not think we are alone in this universe."

"Are you saying that aliens are demons?"

"Ghosts, demons, devils, fantasmas, diablos, spirits, sprites, creatures from other dimensions, other planets; if they are not humanos, they are aliens," don Rojas replied. "And sometimes they take possession of a human to do evil."

"How? Why?"

"They enjoy it. It can be a game. Even wars can be a game played by gods and demonios."

"How do you know this?" I asked. "Or are you just speculating?"

"Even the gods have gods who have gods," he replied cryptically.

I pulled back onto the highway. This guy was blowing my mind!

"You said you were waiting for me. How'd you know I was coming?" I asked.

"Waiting? No. You arrived before me," he answered. "And there are only a few highways in Sonora. It was easy to figure out where you've been, where you are going."

"I don't understand," I muttered.

don Rojas laughed. "People talk. Word gets around. You made a big impression, visiting so many villages with all your bothersome questions and your long hair. Some feared you may be a demonio or a Brujo, a sorcerer of black magico."

"That's crazy!" I answered. I accelerated and put the car in 4th gear. "Me? A demon? A Brujo? I never gave anyone that impression. Why would anyone think that?"

He stared intently, studying me. "Because maybe you are not of this Earth," he said.

"Bull shit," I answered.

"Language," don Rojas interrupted, "contains words of power; energía positiva y energía negativa. A man of knowledge, of wisdom, a man who sees, would be careful before uttering such words as they are auto-destructivo; they suck energy from the mind, the soul, alma, making the warrior weak."

I began to slow down again, thinking, feel confused.

"Keep driving," don Rojas encouraged. "The wind feels good on my face."

"Okay. How am I not of this Earth?"

"Perhaps you are already dead; the ghost of a boy who died a long time ago."

"What the fuck? What are you talking about?" I asked. But I knew the answer: I died when I was three years old, suffocated, choked to death on a peanut. But the doctors brought me back to life. That's when I first saw the Three Luminous Beings hovering over my hospital bed.

don Rojas smiled at me: "Have you ever suspected, my gringo amigo, that you are a cosmic accident and not supposed to exist in this layer of reality?"

"What the fuck!?" I stated emphatically, my face a frown.

"Perhaps you died, and a black sorcerer conjured you forth from a separate reality."

"And why would a sorcerer do that? Why would you even think this?" I demanded.

"Oh, it is not I, who thinks this; but a little bird who whispered in my ear. So, I decided to see."

I looked at don Rojas who was watching intently, studying me.

"I am not a demon. I am not dead. I am here. I exist. No demon or Brujo conjured me up," I stated emphatically. "And I am not a Brujo. At least, not yet."

"Yes, I can see," don Rojas replied.

"I read this book" I said, holding it up. "This is why I'm here, in Sonora. I am searching for the key to the door that leads to a separate reality. I believe don Juan, or a Brujo, can help me."

don Rojas gazed at me questioningly. "But those with power are using you, are they not?"

I kept my eyes on the road, thinking. Did he know about The Company? Impossible.

"I'm my own boss. Maybe its me who's using those with power," I replied.

don Rojas, never taking his eyes from me, reached into his bag: "I have in here flowers, plants, herbs, peyote, mushrooms, God's Flesh, the keys and the doors to those separate realities. You are not ready to open those doors."

"Not ready? Why? What could happen?" I asked.

"Because, if you pass through those doors, you may not come back," he replied.

"Why's that?" I asked.

"You are weak, easily conquered by lust. The illusion of a woman's beauty will lead you astray," he answered. "And there are many beautiful demonios."

"I am willing to risk that chance," I answered. "And I've taken LSD and chewed peyote. I also meditate and practice Yoga. I've been to places in the mind most people don't even know exist."

"Yes, I can see," don Rojas replied. "You are different from the others. You seek, you know of these realities without understanding their nature. You are a warrior, yet you are lost, in need of a guide. You will make great discoveries which can never be acknowledged in this world because you do not exist. You died. You are not supposed to be here. You are a cosmic accident. I can see all this. But why did you survive? Why did you come back to life? These are my questions. I too am a seeker of knowledge which is power. This is why I asked to ride with you."

"For what purpose?" I asked.

"Teachers must teach," he answered. "Or they lose their purpose and cease to exist. A teacher must learn, or he cannot teach. I may learn something from a man who died but lives and should not be here."

"You're offering to teach me?" I asked. "Are you a sorcerer?"

don Rojas ignored my questions and just smiled.

I sped up, deep in thought: cactus to the left of me, cactus to the right, and the occasional rotting corpse of some animal smashed flat by a passing car or truck.

"Tell me," I asked. "If you'd decided I was a demon, what would you have done?

don Rojas became very serious: "I would have sent you back to the hell from which you had come."

"You were planning to kill me?"

"No. I came to see. To learn. You interest me. And now, my gringo amigo, we shall take a journey together, along this road in this fine new automobile. But, our real journey begins with a little smoke."

From within his brown leather bag, don Rojas retrieved a small oblong wooden box which contained a pipe carved out of bone. He unbuttoned the throat of his shirt and detached three small leather satchels which hung from his neck by leather straps.

From each of the little satchels he retrieved a pinch of a flowery mixture which he inserted, as a series of layers, into the pipe. Lighting the pipe, he inhaled deeply.

"I'd like some of that..." I said, but he interrupted by blowing a cloud of smoke in my face.

"Just drive," he replied. "The little smoke will take us to our destination."

Suddenly, my heart was racing, my breathing accelerating, and the landscape rushing by at an increasing pace as if my "VW" was doing 150 miles per hour and speeding up. Impossible!

The surroundings become a rushing blur. The sun appeared to be falling! I could see it setting, faster, faster... and not just the sun but my thoughts were racing, as were my answers to don Rojas' questions which he fired off at a dizzying pace.

Time was speeding up, becoming compressed. One moment it was three in the afternoon and... then it was dusk and just as suddenly a billion stars were twinkling up above.

And when not questioning, he was teaching: "Tetlachiwikes can sicken or kill their victim by touch or the stare of an evil eye." "Tlawkpochimes are evil witches, almost always women, who remain young by killing and drinking the blood of virgins and young babies." "Tetzitacs are almost always men and can control the weather, bring rain, hail, or snow." "Nahuatls are shape-shifters and can become birds, beasts, rocks, plants and can assume the shape of other humans." "Tetlachihuics are true sorcerers and have all these powers, and more. They can heal the sick, travel through time, and are often called upon, and paid for their services, by those in need of a cure, some white magic."

"Are you a Tetlachihuics?" I asked.

don Rojas merely shrugged.

"You said you can cure. Is that true" I asked.

"Si. Cure, cast off evil spells, exorcise demonios."

"And you get paid for this?" I asked.

He laughed. "Si. I have become very wealthy by doing good."

"You make money being a sorcerer?" I asked, disbelieving. "I thought sorcerers lived like hermits and cared nothing for money."

don Rojas explained: "Only those with little power, or who are crazed, loco, possessed, or consumed by evil, remain poor. Power is money. Money is power. The more power, the greater the wealth. Those afflicted by disease, or who are cursed by the evil ones, pay good money to be cured, to send the spells back to where they came. Power is control, and even sorcerers, if they are not wary, if their true names are known, can be controlled," he said with a flourish.

Can a Tetlachihuic control those in power? Kings? Queens? Presidents?" I asked.

"Influence, yes, depending on the distance. If the Tetlachihuic has bits of hair, clothing, feces, nail clippings; the greater the power."

"And you do this by casting a spell? By using Voodoo?" I asked.

"By the power of inner vision. By creating a mental image of that man, or woman, and making them, the image, do what you desire, at that moment. They become a puppet dancing in a parallel reality in the mind's eye."

I thought of the old crone in the medicine booth, with the dead blind eyes. I though for sure she may have been a witch casting a spell.

"Can a woman become a Tetlachihuic?" I asked.

"One is born a Tetlachihuic. Power can be absorbed, enhanced by herbs, spells, medicinal plants, Teo-nanacatl, and by learning; like exercising a muscle. But yes, women, my mother, my wife, my daughter, were born Tetlachihuics."

"You're married? You have children?" I asked, surprised. "A sorcerer with a family. Wow. Far Out! Never thought of that before," I admitted.

"Even Jesus was married," don Rojas replied. "Jesus, Mary Magdalena, both were Tetlachihuics and had children."

"How do you know that?" I asked.

"What I do know is Tetlachihuics are the most powerful of all sorcerers, and the women are the most dangerous."

"Why's that?" I asked.

"Jealousies. Crazy love. Sexual desire. Women are smarter than most men. Inteligente! They are devious, cunning and mask it with a smile or by pretending to be weak; and they are more emotional, irrational and may wish death even to those they love. They may kiss their best friend on the cheek, and stab her in the back at the same time. Even the Devil fears his wife."

"Your daughter is a Tetlachihuic ?" I asked.

"Yes, but she is very powerful, dangerous."

"How so?" I asked. "Is she evil?"

"Is the lion who eats the lamb, evil?" he asked with a smile.

"Well, if you're the lamb, yeah. Evil," I replied.

"My daughter is all woman," don Rojas explained. "Women are dangerous. Use sex as a weapon. Worship their youth. Vanity thy name is woman."

"Are you saying women are evil?"

don Rojas laughed: "Angel's face. Devil's heart. No, my daughter is not evil. Remember. Women are smarter than most men who are easily tricked by a beautiful woman. My daughter, she stays young and grows stronger, more powerful, by entrancing men with her beauty and sucking away the power of foolish men who dare to love her. All women do the same. This is why, my amigo gringo, you must never fall in love with and never make love to my daughter. If you do, you shall be cast from the garden of Eden and the fruit from the Tree of Knowledge may be lost to you, forever."

And now the moon was rising, shadowing trees in silhouette.

"Slow down!" don Rojas commanded with a clap of his hands. "There's a turn off, up ahead. We will take that road."

I slowed down. Everything slowed down.

"Where are we going?" I asked.

"My hacienda. Stop. Stop. Now turn to the right," he commanded.

There was a full moon and the landscape was illuminated with an eerie moon-light glow. I couldn't see any turnoff. No intersection. Just trees, scrub oaks, pines.

"But there's no road," I complained. "That looks like a gully, maybe a canyon!"

"It is," he answered.

"What if the car gets stuck in the sand?"

"It won't."

Slowly, gingerly, I maneuvered my VW over the rugged and rocky terrain, then down a gentle slope which led to a one lane hard packed dirt road on either side of which were an increasing number of trees.

"Follow the road. Keep driving," don Rojas said reassuringly.

We came to a river and a wooden bridge. On the other side a one lane paved road bounded by lush vegetation and a variety of oak, pine, and deciduous trees. don Rojas directed me to keep following the road.

"I'm feeling a bit confused," I admitted. "After I picked you up time went by very fast. I don't understand what's happened. It was like time speeded up. Seems like five hours went by in five minutes."

don Rojas laughed. "It's the little smoke," he replied. "My special blend. I call it, conciencia a la velocidad de la luz."

"Consciousness at the speed of light?" I repeated giving him a questioning look.

"Si. Two more puffs and consciousness would accelerate so fast we would have headed back into the past."

"So you're saying the smoke made us jump into the future?" I asked.

"Not jump. The little smoke made consciousness go faster which made what we experience as time, contract. Have you heard of the reading a book, very fast? Lectura veloz?"

"Speed reading? Sure," I answered.

"The little smoke was like speed reading the pages of time, consciousness at the speed of light. Four puffs and we would have gone so fast along that silver string we would have visited the future and ended up in the past. And this too gives the Sorcerer great power. A Sorcerer may change his past, and his future."

"The sliver string?"

"Yes, and it stretches from your navel, across the years of time, from the moment you were conceived to the moment you die. Pluck the string, and time vibrates into your future and your past. Time, is a circle. Future, past, now, all a circle."

"And a sorcerer can travel to the future?" I asked.

"We all travel to the future. But a sorcerer, if he has you in his grip, or with a touch, or a kiss, can also take you into the future, or back in time, into the past."

The landscape on the other side of yet another bridge had been farmed and there were a variety of growing crops. We came upon rows of corn, squash, melons, which don Rojas told me were fed by irrigation ditches leading from the river.

"Do you own all this? Is this your land?" I asked.

don Rojas laughed. "Typical Gringo question. How can anyone own land? Its like asking if I own the sky, or the clouds. We are almost to the Hacienda."

I spied an ancient dilapidated wooden barn and a mud-brick hovel which was in such bad shape, leaning at impossible angles, I was sure a strong wind could easily knock it down.

"Nice place you have here, Mr. don Rojas," I said and laughed.

"Those are memories. The hacienda is just over that rise, hidden by the trees. See the glow? Follow the light," he instructed, and I did.

I was stunned. The hacienda was huge, magnificent, castle-like. Two stories, all lit up with lanterns and what looked like electric lights... and there was a fountain and a large circular brick driveway with pickup trucks and jeeps parked out front.

There were also a number of outbuildings, five car garage, huge barn, corral, stable for horses, hutches and pens for the farm animals, and fruiting trees and well tended gardens.

"This is all yours?" I sputtered as I climbed out of my car, my mouth agape.

"Yes," he replied modestly.

Seven big dogs ran up, all but two happily wagging their tales, exuding joy at the return of their master; and two growling under the breath, signally they did not like me at all.

don Rojas patted their heads, scratched their eyes, and off they ran.

"Those dogs look like wolves," I said.

He didn't answer, but instead led me around the hacienda. It felt good to stretch my legs.

Even more surprising: a huge circular spiral antenna on the roof and two more set up to the far left of the hacienda.

"And what are those for?" I asked, pointing at the spiral antenna. "I thought only NASA had those things."

"Satellite dishes," he explained. "My ninos, the first born in December of 1962. Added those over there in 1965 and 1967. Keeps me informed. El conocimiento es poder! El conocimiento es poder!"

"Where do you get the electricity?"

"River turbines. Solar power. Gas generators."

"How do you pay for all this?" I asked.

"Deniro. Lots of money."

He led me to a well lit courtyard. A beautiful young woman stepped out of the hacienda into the light. She wasn't smiling.

I was stunned. Eyes of fire, lips of desire! It was her! Or her identical twin! The same cursing beauty who chased me from the village square that same morning.

"You should have killed him," she said, then turned, and with a sway of her hips, strolled back toward the hacienda; but not before stopping, gazing over her shoulder, and giving me an enticing smile.

My dick was standing straight up at attention. What a delicious babe! Foxy Lady!

"You have been struck by the thunderbolt," don Rojas laughed. "But remember," he continued, turning serious. "Beware paradise lost, so take care, or you will be cast from Eden!"

Eden? What was he talking about? I knew paradise when I saw it: and it was right between her legs.

don Rojas took me by the arm and led me through the stained glass double door entrance of the big hacienda. We were greeted by an old lady, a housekeeper. He instructed her to bring an evening meal and to prepare a bedroom for his guest, meaning yours truly.

The interior of the hacienda was magnificent. Antique furniture, marble and terracotta statues, wood and ebony carvings of magical beasts, exquisitely painted pottery and porcelain, brilliant paintings by artists famous and unknown. It was like stepping into a museum.

"Wow! This place blows my mind." I said. "Totally out of sight! But, I'd think a real Sorcerer wouldn't be into all this materialism."

don Rojas laughed. "Every world, every reality, has its own materiality which differs from the rest. We live in a materialistic world. We eat, shit, keep warm, and do what we can to live comfortably. Yes, its all an illusion. We all have our illusions. I happen to enjoy my illusions without being controlled by them."

"You got all this using sorcery?" I asked.

"Knowledge is power," he answered. "Power is money."

I looked at him askance. Was don Rojas some far out crazy rich guy totally off his nut, or the real deal? I wasn't sure what to believe.

don Rojas laughed. "Tell me," he replied, "Why would a sorcerer, a man of power, live like a peasant? True, some do, but only because the power, the ability to see, brujería, made them loco. So they withdraw from the world and live like ermitaños en un agujero de mierda,"

Yet another room was one massive library. From floor to ceiling, row upon row of well stocked shelves bursting with books, parchments, and scrolls, many extremely ancient.

"Wow. Far out! Have you read all these books?" I asked.

"Not all. Many are for reference."

Then another spacious, ornate and richly furnished room, but crowded with musical instruments, horns, a clavichord, harps, drums, and those the likes of which I'd never seen before.

"I didn't realize you were a musician too," I said, admiring his collection.

"These are for magico," he answered. "La música of the spheres."

"Magic?" I asked. "In what way?"

don Rojas laughed: "All music, good music, can be magical, and transport us to other worlds."

The old lady housekeeper appeared and indicated dinner and my room were ready.

"Will your daughter be joining us for dinner?" I asked.

"Perhaps," he answered.

"And what about your wife?"

don Rojas' smile disappeared.

"She is dead," announced don Rojas's daughter as she entered the dining room. "Killed by a jealous Tetlachihuic. My father, with his roving eye, is to blame."

She strolled boldly across the room, her fiery eyes blazing. "I am Sophia," she said, offering me the back of her hand to kiss. "We have already met twice, earlier this day."

I took her hand, her fingers long slim, elegant. Turning it over, I kissed her palm. The feeling was electric. Surprised, she pulled her hand away, and then stared at me curiously her green eyes flashing with curiosity and a hint of desire.

"You say we met twice?" I asked. "No, I would remember you. We only met once. And, you were not very nice."

"That's because," she said airily, "I did not know what you are. Now I see," she laughed wickedly, "you can't even see."

"But he has power," don Rojas replied.

"Does he?" she said, looking at me with growing curiosity.

"Yes, and he has seen the Trinidad from the other side."

I looked at him with surprise. Did I really tell him about those three entities?

During dinner, which was absolutely delicious, and in reply to my questions about music and magic, don Rojas explained that certain sounds and frequencies have physical properties, which, he said, interact with the "cosmic energy that enclose and keep the parallel realities separate and apart."

"Sounds can make holes in the cosmic barriers, and make the holes grow larger," he explained. "A sorcerer, if he has courage, may cross over into another reality through the holes he makes. He may also be taken captive by demons, and not come back."

"Well, that's a vacation I'd rather not take," I replied.

Throughout dinner, don Rojas and Sophia would sometimes surreptitiously observe me as I tried certain foods from the numerous side dishes or drank from my glass; which led me to wonder about drugs or poison. But, there was nothing sinister about their behavior. On the contrary, don Rojas was a friendly gracious host, and Sophia was surprisingly intelligent, articulate, knowledgeable, and, flirtatious. When I caught her eye, she'd smile, laugh or boldly stare and ask: "What?"

Eyes of fire, lips of desire! A slim but curvaceous body that begs to be hugged and squeezed! Hot damn she was a beautiful babe. What a fox! This is a woman I'd happily eat for dinner, and for desert too! Of course, I kept those thoughts to myself.

Dinner over, don Rojas slid his chair from the table, and said: "You are tired. Let us rest, sleep. Dream. We will continue our journey in the morning."

"Where are we going?" I asked.

"To another reality," he replied.

I wasn't tired, and wanted to go for a long walk, stretch my legs and think. Sophia, to my delight, offered to escort me.

"Otherwise you may get lost, my handsome gringo man," she teased.

don Rojas gave me a look of concern as he ascended a spiral stairway to the upstairs bedrooms. "Remember, my gringo amigo: Beware paradise lost! Sí. Its the truth. So watch out."

Paradise? I was looking at her!

Sophia and I strolled together in the moonlight. It was very romantic. To my delight, Sophia said to me: "You may hold my hand."

Her skin was cool, smooth, electric, our fingers entwined as if we had always been two hearts, now joined together as one. Wow. I really liked this woman!

We came upon some cats sitting in a circle, a fox slinking off into the moonlight followed by a hopping rabbit. Two hooting owls turned their heads 180 degrees following us with their eyes, three goats stood their ground and stared, and a parade of mice in rows of two slowly made their way toward a well kept barn, in the shadows of which I could see lots of glowing eyes.

And was that a mountain lion, maybe a jaguar, sitting, lying in the distant shadows, watching? I was about to point them out and ask, when seven big hairy dog-like-wolves came bounding up, a few snarling, the rest wagging tails, happy to greet us; a repeat performance from when I first arrived. Sophia scratched their ears, patted their heads, and contented and happy they turned and went their way.

"Lots of animals roaming around here," I said casually.

"Helpers. Servants. Familiars. Workers," she replied, then added: "And visitors. They come, they go."

I wasn't sure what the hell she was talking about, but kept my questions to myself, staying focused entirely on enjoying her company. I really liked this girl!

Side by side we continued to stroll, holding hands, basking in the moonlight. The air was moist, the evening temperatures just right. I could smell the river. A gentle mist was settling over the moonlit landscape. It was magical, beautiful, enchanting... and... she asked about the "Trinidad" so I told her of my experience.

She was sweet, affectionate, squeezing my hand, leaning close next to my side.

"Its hard to believe you're the same woman who chased me away this morning," I said, gazing into her emerald eyes.

"I'm a shape-shifter," she replied.

"I like your shape," I answered.

"Shape shifting is how my mother died," she said softly. "Terranza killed her."

"Terranza? What's that? I don't understand," I replied.

"My father has a wondering eye. Never faithful. He's had many lovers; some of whom he'd love, then cast away, a ship passing in the night. Terranza was his lover. But Terranza was a Tetlachihuic. Jealous of my mother. Angry with my father. Terranza did not like to be trifled with."

"What happened?" I asked.

"Tetlachihuics can die. We can be killed. Shape shifting takes power, drains energy, and can make a Tetlachihuic weak, like an old woman when retaking human form. One needs a few moments, magic, power, to recover."

"My mother was flying high, she had become an Eagle, soaring through the sky to rendezvous with my father. A hunter's gun, in the power of Terranza, shot my mother. Wounded, my mother took human shape, fell from the sky, upon the earth, and died."

Strolling in the moonlight, I tenderly squeezed Sophia's hand and gave her a look of sympathy--though, in truth, I didn't believe a word. It was all too fantastic. We slowed our pace and stopped beside my car.

"And what happened to Terranza?" I asked.

"My father, and I, together, we combined our powers. Casting spells, calling her secret name, we shape-shifted Terranza into a spider, which we captured, then starved to death inside a glass jar."

"I told my father," Sophia added, "we should kill Terranza's son, an evil man who is a padre to diablo. We must change him too, into a spider, or he may seek revenge, I said to my father. But, he say, no, the man did my mother no harm and he has little power."

Tuning people into spiders? What nonsense, what a crazy chick, I thought, and almost laughed, but masked my disbelief by changing the subject.

"Want to go for a ride?" I asked.

"You don't believe me," she said, pulling her hand away. "You are a child. You don't know how to see."

"Seeing is believing," I replied.

"Then see," she demanded.

"Okay. Show me," I challenged. "Change into an eagle."

"Too dangerous," she answered. "I prefer blackbirds, ravens, hawks. No one pays them attention, and there's little risk of being shot by a hunter's gun."

"Okay. Do it," I challenged.

In reply, Sophia leaned close and kissed me deeply, passionately, her darting tongue exploring. My mind exploded with light... I was flying...soaring through the air, gliding with the wind... I could see the desert, then a village down below... an open air market... a gringo, me, moving through the crowds... I glided downwards, and landed with a flap of my wings, which became a black feathered fan, and stood at a booth gazing at the magical herbs and potions, aware of the handsome gringo appraising me with heart throbbing desire...

I pulled away from Sophia's eager red lips and gazed at her with excited confusion.

"How'd you do that?" I demanded.

"The silver thread," she replied, her eyes flashing. "A Tetlachihuic can travel backwards in time."

"Fucking A! That was far out amazing!" I exclaimed.

Sophia took my hands, leaned close, her breasts pressing against my chest, and whispered tiny kisses in my ear sending tingles of electric delight up and down my spine.

"I can take you higher," she promised.

To my astonished delight, she dropped down to her knees, and while gazing innocently upwards into my eyes, unbuckled my belt, my pants, and down went the zipper. She pulled out my throbbing cock, stroked it with her fingers, kissed and licked the head, then slipped it into her mouth and began sucking like an angel!

I was in heaven, melting, leaning against my car for support... and then... I pulled my cock from her sucking lips, and turned her over, face down on the hood of my car. My hands slipped beneath her skirt, beneath her panties, squeezing her tight butt, running my fingers between her legs... touching, feeling, exploring... she was wet, gasping with excitement... and I took her from behind, shoving my cock deep inside her... in and out...in and out... faster, deeper...kissing the back of her neck, my arms wrapped around squeezing her breasts... in and out... in and out...

I wanted to shout: I love you.

"You are an amazing lover. I love fucking you," I gasped.

"I can take you higher," she purred, and turning round, she leaned against the car, spread her long legs, held me close, and I was again inside her... kissing her eager lips, squeezing her breasts, her buttocks... feeling her, holding her, loving her... in and out... in and out... deeper... harder... and... we were flying... flying.... higher... higher...the desert down below... cactus, gullies... a highway... hovels in the distance...a graveyard of wrecked cars... flying, flying...soaring across the sky... and I was deep inside her.... and cumming, she was cumming, her long legs wrapped around me, blazing eyes locked onto my own... and... she was milking me with her puss and I kept cumming and cumming... my eyes tightly closed in one final heavenly ecstatic explosion of orgasmic delight...

I was exhausted, drained of energy, and overcome with the need for sleep.

Opening my tired eyes I gazed through the windshield at a black crow standing on the hood of my car. It cocked its head to the left and right staring at me as I stared back.

I turned my head this way and that, looking at my surrounding. I was back at the Pemex gas station. A short, fat sweating woman and two dirty, squirming brats stood in a dilapidated doorway. A tall thin Mexican man was striding toward my car, a dirty rag in his hands.

And then, with a girlish-human-like laugh, the crow flapped its wings, and was gone.

2. Project ULTRA: Assassins, Psychic Warriors, LSD

I sat in my car, exhausted, confused, unsure as to what happened or why. Had the entire experience been a dream? A LSD-induced hallucination?

And who would do this to me? Why? How? There was only one logical, rational explanation: The Company! Was I a victim of ULTRA mind-control?

My weary eyes took in the surroundings. This was no hallucination. It was like deja vu. Everything was familiar; happening exactly as before: the fat woman and the two squirming brats standing at the door of the cantina; the owner walking toward my VW wiping his hands on a dirty rag; the two old men on the bench in the shade of the stacked tires.

I tiredly dragged myself out of the car, exhausted, weak, depressed, decrepit, totally drained of energy; a Methuselah with one foot in the grave.

The owner and I agreed on the price, and yes they sold Coca Cola. He began pumping gas into my VW, his eyes fixated on the nozzle. It was deja vu all over again.

My throat dry, parched, I shuffled slowly toward the cantina, like an old man. A rusted red white and blue "Coca Cola" sign above a dirty cracked window was exactly where I had already seen it. When? A few minutes ago? Yesterday?

Slowly, on tottering, tired legs, I made my way to the entrance; the short fat Mexican woman and her brats stepping aside to let me pass.

Just as before, the place was dark, dirty, dilapidated, and crowded with barrels of flower, sugar, red peppers, assorted tools, cobwebs, dust devils, and sand and dirt on the rotting wooden floor. Faded fly-speckled posters of bull fighters adorned the walls; there were shelves lined with rusty canned goods, cigar boxes and cartons of cigarettes; and sitting on a rustic pine countertop: cellophane wrapped tamales and packages of Hostess cupcakes that had to be a million years old, and four large jars containing candies, chewing gum, pig's feet, and the fourth identity unknown.

A fan hanging from the ceiling swirled slowly without effect. Buzzing flies circled lazily. It was suffocating, stifling hot.

Exactly as before, I spied a large bottle-cap-shaped "Coca Cola" sign hanging on the wall, a picture of Jesus on one side and a poster of a bull fighter flinging his red cape and stabbing a bloodied bull on the other. Beneath the poster were stacked cases of bottled coke next to a red and white ice cooler, also named: "Coca Cola."

Down in Mexico, these Coca Cola signs were as common as a crucifix.

Everything was as remembered, from what seemed like yesterday, but could have only been minutes ago.

What the hell happened to me? If this was a nightmare, or some kind of weird LSD-flashback, I willed it to immediately come to an end. It didn't.

I leaned tiredly on the dusty pine counter. "Coca Cola?" I rasped and slumped down on a wooden bar stool.

The fat woman, sweating like a pig, popped the cap off a coke and poured some of the dark syrupy liquid into a smudged dirty glass.

"No, no, no," I said, shoving the glass across the counter and grabbing thirstily for the bottle.

The woman, reaching beneath the counter, said: "El Señor, te dijo que te diera esto."

"A man left something for me?" I said with surprise. "Quien? Who?"

Opening a small brown satchel she poured the meager contents into my coke, and said: "Tu bebes esto."

"Qué es? What is that stuff?"

"The Señor, he say, you drink," she answered.

I picked up the dirty glass, stared into the black swirling bubbling fluid and put it back on the counter. I gazed questioningly at the fat woman. Beads of sweat were dripping from her brow, down her fat oily cheeks, plopping dangerously close to my now warm glass of Coke.

It was hellishly hot. Why didn't they open a window?

She eyed me warily, impatient.

I was thinking, considering the possibilities: perhaps someone from The Company had slipped me some LSD--which would account for everything; meaning, don Rojas, Sophia, the hacienda, had been a very realistic hallucination. Now someone from The Company arranged for me to drink this crap, which, was, what? An antidote? More LSD? Poison? Dead men tell no tales? No! Poison made no sense. Shooting me, dumping the body, would be a lot easier; except there was no reason to kill me!

The only other possibility was...

"The Señor? His name? Como se llamaba el hombre?" I asked, my voice parched. "Was don Rojas the man who left this for me?"

The woman made the sign of the cross: "Tu bebes esto. You drink," she repeated.

"Qué vertiste en esa Coca?" I asked again. "What did you pour in my Coke?"

"The Señor, he say, you drink," she repeated for the third time.

So, I did, and instantly felt a hell of a lot better, completely awake, energized, my mind crystal clear, my body surging with an electric feeling of vitality, strength, power! The change must have been noticeable. The woman's eyes grew wide, she took a step back, began to make the sign of the cross, but stopped; her wariness replaced by a look of determination.

"Pagas diez dolares Americanos," she demanded, holding out her fat open palm for payment.

"Ten dollars? For a Coke?" I pointed at the sign above the Coca Cola ice chest. "The sign says 8 pesos! Veinticinco centavos."

"Pagas diez dolares Americanos," she insisted.

I paid the ten, then bought another six Cokes from the cooler, 8 pesos each. Cokes in hand I peppered her with questions about "don Rojas." But she said nothing more.

Exiting the cantina, feeling great, I looked around, blinking in the fiendishly hot almost blindingly bright light: No crows, eagles. The two old men gone! And no "don Rojas."

Questioning the tall skinny Mexican as I paid for gas, yielded only a "No comprehende."

Sliding behind the wheel, I wasn't sure what to do. Look for don Rojas? Keep searching for a sorcerer? Give up and go home? No. I'd been warned: Failure was not an option. And who the hell left that stuff for me to drink?

The Sonora sun was cooking my head and my hair felt on fire, so I fetched from the passenger seat my denim cowboy hat to umbrella away the blazing rays. That's when I noticed the brown leather sack partly shoved beneath the seat.

Fuckin' A.

I searched the bag, dumped the contents, and seven small satchels--and an oblong box I knew contained a pipe carved out of bone--fell upon the passenger seat. The pipe was empty. Two little satchels contained magic psilocybin mushrooms and peyote and a third was filled with flowery vines I recognized as "ayahuasca." But whatever was in the other four was a mystery to me.

Did don Rojas stash his magic bag while I was in the cantina? Could he have left it in my car after we arrived at his hacienda? What the hell was going on?

No way he forgot it. don Rojas must have had good reason for leaving me his satchel.

From the glovebox I retrieved a map and began plotting coordinates. I had been traveling south down Highway 15. Having already twice journeyed to Guaymas, I had planned to bypass Hermosilla and take Highway 14. don Rojas said he wanted to go East. That meant highway 14. There were three major rivers nearby: the San Miguel, Sonora, and Montezuma two of which had tributaries that crossed highway 14.

Putting the car in gear I headed East.

What were the possibilities I could find don Rojas and his hacienda? There was no 'little smoke' to guide the way. There was no way could I find the turn off from the highway, of that I was sure. There may have been several turn offs.

What a bummer!

And what if don Rojas doesn't want to be found?

And what do I tell The Company?

Sophia! That's how I ended up back at the Pemex station, feeling weak and drained of energy, like a decrepit old man. Sophia!

don Rojas warned me three time about that girl! I didn't believe him. Thought he was just the typical father protecting the chastity of his precious angel. I'm a fool, a moron. What an idiot!

How could I become a true warrior, a man of knowledge, and open doors to other realities, if I let my dick do the thinking, and am too sex-stupid to listen and learn when warned?

This had been a "problem" since I was first seduced at age 13 by a 21-year-old newlywed --Mrs. T.-- whose lawn I mowed every week. Soon I was mowing more than her lawn. She was a wild cat; insatiable; loved to suck; thought I'd gone to heaven. I remember saying: "your husband is so lucky!" Then the luck ran out when he caught us naked, in bed, me riding her like a pony! Bummer! Still, she was amazing. I was addicted. After that delicious sexcapade, if a woman was good lookin' I immediately thought "sex" and wanted to fuck her! It was a terrible distraction. A weakness. But what unmarried young man can resist a beautiful babe looking for Mr. Right Now? Not me! At least, not back then.

"Beware paradise lost!" "The illusion of a woman's beauty will lead you astray," don Rojas had warned. And it did: Sophia! What a babe! And what a bitch!

Pussy is paradise no doubt about it! But it can also take a man where he doesn't want to go: Heartbreak Hotel, and, Hell.

Stupidly, I knew, if given half the chance, I'd probably do her again.

No! She tricked me. Used me. I'm not going to be manipulated by some sexy witch!

I gave a sidelong glance at the brown leather sack, which I'd stuffed partly beneath the passenger seat, to keep it out of the sun. The keys and doors to a different kind of paradise were within this bag: the ability to explore alternate realities, parallel worlds, and acquire knowledge, power, magic, even cosmic wisdom.

Why did don Rojas leave me his magic bag? Certainly he didn't forget it. Or did he? No. Obviously it's for my use: keys and doors. The fruit of the tree of knowledge! Problem is, what some of this stuff was, what it might do was unknown to me!

Well, there was only one way to find out. Eat it, smoke it. Garden of Eden, Tree of Knowledge, here I come.

Or would that be stupid?

I tried to remember all don Rojas had told me while we were 'speed reading the pages of time', racing to his hacienda guided by the little smoke. I'd have to write everything down. The Company would expect documentation and detailed notes. The log book was in the glove box. But first, I would need a shady place to park. I continued to drive, thinking.

The desert became thorn scrub; and if I was on the right track and memory served me well, a few hours up ahead, I'd encounter deciduous forest, and if lucky, maybe the tributary of a river that would lead me to don Rojas... and... Sophia. Yes, as stupid as it seemed, despite what she'd done to me, I really liked Sophia. A lot. I wanted to see her again.

And how could I not like, honor, and respect don Rojas who offered me friendship and the keys to the doors to other realities? He trusted me!

I felt conflicted. If I found him, what should I do?

I was on the horns of a dilemma which was pricking painfully into the butt-end of my conscience.

General Wheeler's men had offered me what at first seem liked a good deal, and a way to escape certain induction into the Army and death in Vietnam. The "James Bond" "vacation in Mexico" "meet a sorcerer" and "fuck a lot of hot chicks" pitch was too good to be true--and stupidly, I believed them, having no idea, at first, of what they really had in mind.

I accepted a draft deferment, money, a new car, and after months of training, and believing I had no other viable options, agreed to fulfill a top secret mission: Travel to Mexico. Locate a sorcerer: Carlos Castaneda's don Juan. Verify don Juan's powers. Take notes. Pictures. Film everything. Make a map. X-marks the spot! Inform "The Company" which would kidnap, put him in a cage, stick electrodes in his brain, and feed him LSD. Why? National Security! The Company was going to train an army of psychic warriors.

"Failure is not an option" I was warned by a steely eyed fierce looking dude in a General's uniform; whereas success would be rewarded to the tune of $25,000. Money to sing by!

The entire mission, under the auspices of The Company, was part of an experimental project code named "ULTRA."

Before my introduction to ULTRA, I had to first complete seven weeks of intense training in weapons, martial arts, sabotage, stealth raids, ambushes, urban warfare, and assassinations. Up at 3 AM, in bed at 9 PM, sometimes go without sleep for 48 hours; it was a total bummer, made worse by the skin-head gung ho thugs and killers who absolutely hated this "long haired hippie freak" and made seven weeks of my life total hell.

But I'd learned, long before that adventure, when push came to shove, kick ass and aim for the balls. When you have 'em by the balls, their hearts and minds will follow. At the end of six weeks, I'd won some respect, was in the best shape of my life, and even knew how to kill with my thumb and pussy finger.

There followed a cluster-fuck in the jungle highlands of Vietnam, and then back to California and a research Institute in Palo Alto where I underwent two weeks of intense educational training: fundamentals of biochemistry, plant and fungal biology, hallucinogens, phenethylamines, lysergamides, hypnosis, and the proper preparation of field notes.

Much to my chagrin, the director of ULTRA decided I'd be perfect for one of his special projects; which was never part of the deal. Fortunately, I couldn't be hypnotized. They couldn't even make me drowsy. I also refused to take any drugs, not even LSD, at least not under sterile laboratory conditions, and certainly not while under observation by white-coated nerds and geeks.

"Tripping out on LSD while locked up in a small white sterile room with wires attached to my head? Hippie's nightmare." I said. "No way."

Several arguments ensued, and I kept repeating "No!" and "I didn't sign up for this!" and "Call General Wheeler."

After they accepted the fact I wasn't going to be a "guinea pig," was impossible to hypnotize, and unsuitable to become a "Manchurian candidate," my two weeks at the "Institute" turned out to be a mind-blowing, far out trip.

First there was the Artificial Intelligence Lab, where I was introduced to the camera equipped "Shakey the Robot" which looked like a filing cabinet on wheels. No arms, no legs, the camera serving as eyes; and although "Shakey" was supposed to open doors and flick on lights, all it could do was roll around the room on little plastic wheels, go through open doors, or bump into walls, then turn around and go the other way. Still, I was impressed. I'd never seen a robot before, except in the movies.

In yet another laboratory there were rats with an assembly of electrodes and wires buried in their brain. They'd walk in circles when the experimenter turned on a switch. With a click of a second switch the rats turned around and circled in the opposite direction.

"Someday," I was told by Divid, the movie-star handsome Project Manager, "humans will be controlled by this same technology, but without the wires."

"Wow. Far out," I said. "Humans going in circles. Cool!"

"This is just the first step," Mr Handsome replied.

"You know what would be really cool?" I asked.

"What's that?"

"A button that will make a beautiful babe want to fuck like crazy."

"There's already a button for that," David answered. "The clitoris."

The section I was assigned to was code named ULTRA, and run by "The Company." They were experimenting with hypnosis, LSD, mescaline, psilocybin, and a variety of other phenethylamines and lysergamides, for the purposes of mind control: creating programmed assassins and "Psychic Warriors."

Initially, I found the "Psychic Warriors" concept fascinating.

They were using LSD, mescaline, and other drugs to develop psychic abilities such as ESP and "remote viewing" a term I heard for the first time when two physicists, one from Stanford University, visited the facility and explained the concept in terms of "quantum physics."

That evening I visited the Institute's small library and found books by Heisenberg and Neils Borhr, and thus began my fascination with quantum mechanics. There were also a lot of scientific journals, including one called "Brain." Wow--I thought, and grabbed a copy of that as well.

I was no stranger to LSD, having first taken this little miracle drug in 1967, during the "Summer of Love"--an entire tab of "Purple Haze"--manufactured by the maestro of psychadelics, Stanely Owsley; and also the title of Jimmy Hendricks' famous song in which he sings: "Purple Haze blows my mind... Excuse me while I kiss the sky..."

Lysergic acid diethylamide (LSD-25), had been created by Albert Hofmann in 1938. Hoffman first experimented on himself with a dose of 250ug of pure LSD while taking a bicycle ride. He was mesmerized by the incredible colors and the enhancement of his senses:

"Kaleidoscopic, fantastic images surged in on me, alternating, variegated, opening and then closing themselves in circles and spirals, exploding in colored fountains, rearranging and hybridizing themselves in constant flux. It was particularly remarkable how every acoustic perception, such as the sound of a door handle or a passing automobile, became transformed into optical perceptions. Every sound generated a vividly changing image, with its own consistent form and color."

But soon Hofmann felt so overwhelmed he returned to his home:

"My surroundings had now transformed themselves in more terrifying ways. Everything in the room spun around, and the familiar objects and pieces of furniture assumed grotesque, threatening forms. They were in continuous motion, animated, as if driven by an inner restlessness... Every exertion of my will, every attempt to put an end to the disintegration of the outer world and the dissolution of my ego, seemed to be a wasted effort... At times I believed myself to be outside my body, and then perceived clearly, as an outside observer."

What was a "trip" was discovering that some of the Institute staff, including many of the scientists, were eating LSD like candy! Hallucinating on the job!

"Philip" was tall, thin, balding, effeminate, his face cratered with acne--one of the many of PhD LSD-eating eggheads running the place. I was fairly sure Phillip was a homo. He'd already commented on my muscles; had felt my arm while asking if I "worked out" and if I liked musicals and Broadway plays. Even so, he was an interesting guy and happily explained some of the concepts behind the Psychic Warriors project.

"The idea," he said, in his high pitched voice, staring at me bug-eyed through his coke-bottle eye-glasses, "is to take subjects who've demonstrated PSI abilities, for example, Senders, and give them LSD to enhance their thought projecting powers. Likewise, LSD is provided to Receivers, to enhance their thought receptive abilities."

"For what purpose?" I asked.

"Imagine," he said in a voice more feminine than masculine, "a meeting of the world's leaders, where friends and adversaries are in attendance. Now imagine," he continued, "if one of the waiters, waitresses, or presidential staff was a Receiver and could read the minds of our enemies. We could also employ a Sender to send thoughts into the mind of an opponent, or one of his advisors and put ideas in their head. That's the ticket to world domination. Isn't that just amazing!"

"It could also be a great way to get laid," I said. "No jewelry, no expensive dinners, no booze, just keep thinking: pull your panties down, babe; bend over and pull down those panties!"

Phillip looked at me bug eyed and said: "I could never have sex with a woman while on LSD. It would be disgusting."

"Phillip, I suspect you'd find sex with a woman disgusting even if you weren't on LSD."

Under the auspices of project "ULTRA" a lot of what they were doing was absolutely surreal, nightmarish. I wanted nothing to do with it. Some of the men in charge reminded me of Nazis.

On my third afternoon at the "Institute" after they discovered I couldn't be hypnotized, I met with this bespectacled scientist, Gottlieb, who immediately reminded me of Heinrich Himmler, Hitler's right hand man who ran the SS, Gestapo and concentration camps. Gottlieb didn't like me at all. The feeling was mutual.

With two club feet, a slight lisp and a stutter, if this guy had an inferiority complex he did an excellent job of masking it with an air of rigid, overbearing, authoritarian, intellectual superiority. Guys like this, especially if they have power, are dangerous.

Gottlieb ran the assassins program. Dude was a sadist. Just the thought of killing people turned him on: murdering men, women, children, babies, Germans, Russians, Africans, Cuba's Fidel Castro, Presidents and Dictators in Central and South America, and Arabs, lots of Arabs--he fantasized about killing them all. It made him wet. The more nightmarish the death, the more he drooled.

"Our mission," Gottlieb explained, "is to develop and provide the government with every means possible to maim or kill targeted groups, individuals, the leaders of enemy countries, and civilian populations. We will accomplish our mission through the delivery of toxic and lethal biochemical and biological agents, and exposure to deadly viruses and disease laden bacteria."

"Far out," I replied, keeping my true feelings to myself.

Gottlieb, giving me a meaningful look, continued: "Another objective is the deployment of assassins specially trained, through mind control, to sacrifice their own lives for the good of our country," said the spider to the fly. "That's where you come in."

"No. That's where I leave."

Gottlieb turned purple he was so pissed.

As part of its manifest, and as I was led to understand, project ULTRA had a two-fold purpose: to identify potential "Manchurian Candidates" who, via mind control, drugs, and hypnosis, would become trained assassins robotically programmed to do the dirty deed then have no memory of it, or their training. And, the creation of Psychic Warriors: ESP, mind reading, premonitions, clairvoyance, were to be weaponized.

"Peter," a muscular, heavy-set, bearded, white-lab-coated Senior Scientist at the "Institute" played a major role in the Psychic Warriors program--and over the years he'd also eaten a lot of LSD. He'd even lived on San Francisco's Haight street during the 1967 Summer of Love. We immediately hit it off.

One evening Peter offered to show me a two hour movie, a collage, film clips, of some of the experiments they'd conducted.

"A movie? Sure," I said. "Got any popcorn?"

"No, but I have some LSD," he answered.

"No thanks," I said, "Not in this place."

Why not? He asked.

"I'd rather hang myself than drop acid here. Hippies' nightmare! Let's see the movie."

I was stunned. In specially outfitted hotel rooms--in "hotels" owed by The Company-- they filmed prostitutes having sex with "Johns" who'd been secretly dosed with LSD, and placed them in varying situations where knives, guns, and ropes for strangling had been strategically placed. The doors were always locked. There was no escape, except through an open window six stories above ground. Sometimes it was the hooker who was high. In some clips, through a hidden audio-speaker, an experimenter urged the "John" --now flying high on LSD-- to "kill her" or "kill yourself." And sometimes, that's what happened. And that's not all!

Self-mutilation, screaming men tearing out their own eyeballs, eating their fingers, stabbing themselves in the head, ripping the skin from their own face... It was sick stuff: snuff films starring insane hallucinating maniacs totally whacked out on LSD.

"We've been giving these guys doses of 1000 to 5000 micrograms," Peter admitted.

"5000 micrograms? Wow, that's heavy," I replied. "I'm surprised their heads didn't explode. When I took 1000 micrograms, I could see through my hand."

In other experiments, they gave high doses of LSD to homosexuals, mental patients, bums off the street, runaway kids, soldiers, college students, even fellow scientists and technicians, then locked them in a room, sometimes in pairs or groups of three or more, and piped in strange sounds, screams, the cries of wild animals, or via a hidden movie camera, projected some really sick shit on the walls, while simultaneously filming the consequences.

It was fascinating and nightmarish.

"How'd you get them to volunteer?" I asked.

"They weren't volunteers," he answered.

Fuckin' A! Bummer!

Yet other experiments featured men, often crying or screaming in terror, sometimes open mouthed and serene, a few rigid and catatonic; strapped in chairs with wires and electrodes attached to their heads. Peter even made an appearance in one clip, adjusting the electrodes attached to the head of one screaming subject. Peter not only ran the experiments but was a whiz at electronics.

Peter explained: "We've also used psychiatric patients, anyone who's hearing voices or suffering from visual hallucinations. The idea is, maybe the voices are real, this is why they go crazy. Maybe its some form of ESP and they're hearing other people's thoughts. If the voices or visions are real, then we want to tap into and develop these abilities."

Peter also told me, they'd dosed with LSD "men, women, and children who'd been severely sexually abused, and soldiers suffering from shell shock."

"Why?" I asked.

"Some of these people have dissociative experiences, like floating outside their body," he explained. "They're perfect candidates for the 'viewing at a distance' experiments."

"What's viewing at a distance?" I asked.

"Many of those who've died and come back to life, report they've flown through the air, and visited distant places," he answered. "Some people who are severely emotionally traumatized, or repeatedly sexually abused, also have dissociative experiences, and may float away when its happening to them."

"You mean, their actual body will fly through the air?" I asked.

"No. Not the body. We believe their personal consciousness, or soul, leaves the body. The same phenomenon can be induced by LSD! This is an ability we wish to develop, harness and control. These subjects would make the perfect spy; they could travel though walls, into secret rooms, go anywhere."

"Is that the same as 'remote viewing?" I asked.

"Same concept, yes," Peter answered. "The remote viewer might be able to see into locked offices, filing cabinets, secret laboratories, brief cases, the inside of letters and suit pockets, and so on, and spy on and observe everything that's happening behind closed doors."

"Such as watching beautiful babes taking off their clothes?" I asked.

Peter laughed. "I'll drink to that."

"How does this apply to quantum mechanics?" I asked.

"Don't know," he answered. "We've been recruiting psychics, or those who claim to be witches, warlocks, or wizards, and paying them big bucks to participate. The goal is to use LSD and other drugs on those who already have some psychic or paranormal abilities, to help develop ESP, mind reading, clairvoyance, and deja vu of future events. The ultimate goal is to train an army of Psychic Warriors."

"Heavy. Far out," I said.

Peter gave me a look: "What confuses me, is, why are you here? You don't fit the stereotype. You don't have any psychic abilities, or do you?"

"No, not really," I lied. Although I kept it to myself and said nothing to Peter or the others, I've often been able to sense things of some importance or significance before they happen, usually that same day, but sometimes even days in advance. But I saw no reason to tell these guys.

"Gottlieb was pissed off because I couldn't be hypnotized," I said.

Peter explained: "He's looking for assassins. Men and women, and especially boys and girls who are easily hypnotized, who've been traumatized; these are the perfect Manchurian Candidates. They pick some of these people when they're children, orphans, if they fit the criteria. It's a good idea to start the drugs and hypnosis early while the mind's still malleable."

"Perfect for what?" I asked. "To become assassins?"

Peter looked around the laboratory, and said: "Let's take a ride; go for a walk."

Once outside, strolling along the rolling Palo Alto hills, Peter pulled a card-sized packet from his laboratory coat pocket, and handed it to me.

There were twelve plastic wrapped blue-colored pills punched into the card. I read the label: "Sandoz."

"Its LSD, want to do a tab?" he asked. "Its super powerful. High quality. Very high dose. 1000 micrograms. Best to take only a quarter tab."

"Tempting, but no," I said. " I'd still be tripping when we get back to the Institute."

In fact, it would be nightmarish. I slept in a locked dorm not far from the Institute, in a small sterile room with white walls, a porcelain toilet and sink, and an uncomfortable mattress to torture me at night. That same dorm also housed some of the nut-cases taking part in Project ULTRA. Take LSD and be stuck there later? No way Jose.

Instead, I removed several of the blue pills and put them in my wallet intending to save them for another day.

Peter retrieved the Sandoz package and popped an entire tablet in his mouth. "Don't mind if I do," he said. "Breakfast of Champions."

"You were saying about assassins?" I asked.

"You've heard of Oswald, right? And Sirhan Sirhan, the guys who killed the Kennedys?" he asked, giving me a serious look.

"Of course."

Peter glanced warily all around, checking to see if we'd been followed, if anyone was listening. It was totally safe. Even the cows were ignoring us.

"Both of them," he said, "Sirhan and Oswald. Manchurian candidates; courtesy of Project UTLRA."

"Manchurian Candidates? You mean like in the movie?" I asked.

"Yeah, that's the ticket," Peter confirmed.

I'd read the book and seen the movie. The Manchurian Candidate was about American POWs captured during the Korean war and brainwashed in North Korea, all of whom had been hypnotized, after repeated traumatic experiences. One of the POWs becomes a sleeper agent, an assassin who, after he returned to the USA, was programmed to kill when a 'handler" reactivates the sleeper-agent's hypnotic state with a post-hypnotic trigger.

"Oswald was a Manchurian Candidate?" I asked, disbelieving. "Man, you've been taking too much LSD," I said. "That's bull shit."

"Jack Ruby, also a project ULTRA success story."

"Bovine feces," I retorted. "You're hallucinating."

"Oswald was perfect," Peter explained. "He'd been traumatized as a kid, had lots of emotional problems, and at age 13 was diagnosed as suffering from a schizoid personality and living in a fantasy. He turned out to be easily hypnotized. ULTRA began the serious mind control and hypnosis experiments after Oswald joined the Marines and was stationed at Atsugi Naval Air base in Japan which is a hot bed of ULTRA activity. Radar, radio waves, electromagnetic waves, that's the future of mind control."

"Anyway, after turning Oswald into an easily hypnotized assassin," Peter continued, "ULTRA sent him to Russia, loaded with key words to trigger different hypnotic killing behaviors. He was easily programmed. All it would take is a phone call, or a stranger on the street, saying the magic word, and Oswald would do as programmed and kill our target. He was the ideal Manchurian candidate!"

"Did he kill anyone in Russia?" I asked.

"No. Russia was a cover to give him bona fides as a Commie. The goal was to get him into Cuba, to kill Castro. But after the Bay of Pigs fiasco, when Kennedy proved himself soft on the commies, and, made the ultimate mistake by firing CIA director Dulles, The Company came up with a new assignment: Kill President Kennedy. That's when ULTRA started a new training regimen using Oswald who was part of a four man hit team: triangulation. He was the patsy. Somebody had to take the blame. Otherwise there'd be an investigation. And guess who would be in charge of the investigation into Kenned's assassination? Dulles. But there was always the danger Oswald might begin to remember. That's where Jack Ruby came into play."

"How do you know this?" I demanded. "Or are you just speculating?"

"Gottlieb. Helms. Dulles. Every room, every lab, every office at the Institute, is wired for sound--and not everyone knows it. But I do. I listened," Peter explained, his voice becoming slurred. "Gottlieb hated the Kennedys, because the father, the old man, Joe Kennedy was a NAZI sympathizer."

"No way. Gottlieb doesn't have the power to kill a President," I argued. "And why should Gottlieb care about Nazis? They lost the war 25 years ago!"

"Never forgive. Never forget. That's... their motto," Peter said, gazing into the sky, his voice soft almost a whisper.

"Whose motto? The Company? Project ULTRA? What are you talking about?"

"That's where... where... Helms and Dulles... come in," Peter explained, pupils dilated, his voice rising and falling in pitch. "Kennedy... fired Dulles who was was was the the the head of the CIA which has on the payroll the best assassins in the the the world. Think that was smart? Think Dulles was was was happy, about, being, fired? Fire the guy guy guy in charge of of of thousands of assassins?"

"Why did Kennedy fires Dulles?" I asked.

"Because of... wow... because of... the...colors... because of the Bay of Pigs... pigs fiasco. Guess, who, investigated... Kenned's... assassination? Dulles," Peter said, answering his own question as he bent down to pluck a blade of grass. "And, who, who, who... get's, the, blame? Oswald..."

"You overheard this?" I asked. "Or did you take part in it?"

Peter held up the grass bade. "Look. It's, glowing, pulsating, I, can, taste, taste, taste it through, my, fingers," he said, handing it to me.

"Were you part of this assassin program?" I asked again.

"That cow," Peter remarked. "It's... listening."

"Not likely," I replied.

"That God damned cow's turning green, blue, purple. Look," he said pointing. "Oh wow, trails," he exclaimed, waving his arm.

"Who is Helms?" I asked.

"Richard...Richard... Helms... in... charge... of... ULTRA. Helms--wow, wow, you're melting," Peter said, staring at me, fascinated.

What about Richard Helms?" I asked.

"Runs ULTRA... runs CIA," Peter said. "You're, melting, turning, into, molecules."

"Sirhan Sirhan killed Robert Kennedy," I said. "How could the CIA have anything to do with that? And why would they?" I asked.

"Sirhan Sirhan... good candidate...easily, hypnotized... female, controller... three, man, hit, team. Wow, now, I'm, melting," Peter exclaimed, staring at his hand, his voice rising several octaves.

It took another five minutes to get the story out of Peter: Sirhan Sirhan had been identified as a possible Manchurian Candidate after he attended an occult psychic meditation event monitored by ULTRA. Sirhan was not very bright with lots of traumas in his past, and one of the most easily hypnotized subjects they'd ever encountered. Sirhan was assigned a sexy female hypnotist/controller and a male trainer (and supposed friend) who hypnotized and taught a hypnotized

Sirhan how to kill Robert Kennedy at point blank range in response to a post-hypnotic code-word and visual trigger (a polka dotted dress) which was to be worn and uttered by the female controller. While hypnotized and in response to a code-word, uttered by the female Controller in a polka dotted dress, Sirhan would instantly become hypnotized and was trained to step up to a Robert Kennedy mannequin and shoot Kennedy in the head, then have no memory of the dastardly deed or why he did it. That Sirhan was an Arab also fitted nicely into The Company's long range plans for the oil rich Middle East.

Did I believe any of this actually happened? I wouldn't be surprise if Dulles and the CIA killed President Kennedy. But this Manchurian candidate business? Not really.

Peter was obviously brilliant, but he was not only eating LSD like candy, but snorting cocaine, and smoking opium, pot, hashish. His brain was addled, no doubt about it. Far as I knew, the entire Sirhan Oswald 'Manchurian Candidate' scenario was a job-related LSD-fantasy.

"But why take out Robert Kennedy?" I asked.

Peter didn't say anything. He was staring at the cow.

"Hey. Peter! Earth to Peter," I said, grabbing his arm to get his attention. "Why would they want to kill Robert Kennedy?"

"Trails. Do... you... see... the... trails?" Peter asked, waving his hand. "Look, I've... got a million... arms."

"Earth to Space!" I said. "Peter, why kill Robert Kennedy?"

"The cow... is... growing horns... like Satan. I think... I think... he's, trying, to, say, something," Peter answered in his increasingly staccato voice.

"Yeah, Moo. Forget the cow. Why did they kill Bobby Kennedy?"

"Who?" Peter asked.

"Rober Kennedy! Senator Kennedy! President Kennedy's brother!"

"Dulles, hated, both, both, both, Kennedys, because of... because of... the cow, cow, cow. They fired Dulles. If, Robert, was, elected, President, might, investigate, Kennedy, assassination. CIA darlings, Senator, Bush, Prescot Bush, Senator, Spook, hated, Kennedys. Wanted, wipe, out, Kennedy, Dynasty," Peter said in his LSD-induced staccato speech.

"Who's Prescot Bush?" I demanded. "Focus. Try to control yourself. Speak English!"

"Senator Spook," Peter replied, still slurring his words. "Rich SOB. CIA. Bush... wants... his... own... dynasty. George, Bush, his, son, CIA, wants to be president, got, to, eliminate, competition, Kennedy Dynasty. Bush, family, big, role, in, putting, together, Kennedy, assassination, hit team... CIA...ULTRA agents... Must, wipe, out, Kennedy, dynasty. They got... Robert Kennedy's kids... addicted... to... drugs... after, they, killed him...turned, Robert's, kids, into, dope addicts... heroin... wipe... out... Kennedy... clan... no more Kennedy dynasty. Bush, dynasty, takes, over. Wow. I am really high. I can see... for miles and...

miles..."

"What about John John? President Kennedy's son? JFK junior?" I asked. "They got him hooked on drugs too?"

"He's... too... protected... some day...Oh wow. The ... colors... alive. I can... taste... the colors... I can... see... my... voice. Look... my, voice, molecules, in, the, air... I'm grooving... every, thing... Psychedelic. Outasite."

"Some day what?" I asked again. "What are they going to do to President Kennedy's son?"

Peter gazed at me unseeing, his eyes as big as silver dollars: "Stop, him... they, know, if, he runs, some, day, he, will, be, elected... They... will... kill.. him.... first... when, he's, still, a, kid, teenager... have accident...maybe, drown, plane, crash... something, not, suspicious... Wow, the... Everything...alive... rocks, clouds, alive... Beautiful... see forever... the sky is opening... look! The sky is breaking into pieces... can see... see heaven, stars... look... look, beyond the sky... stars... I understand... understand why... everything is clear to me... crystal clear... I... know... why... Got the answers... life... death... I can see the face of god..."

The following week, I began receiving need-to-know background information and detailed instructions for my first go-it-alone assignment. My target? A sorcerer: don Juan Matus.

The Company believed that the Russian Commies and Red Chinese, had already made great advances in psychic research and were far ahead of the U.S. in the development of psychic weaponry. The US needed to close the psychic security gap. This was a top priority.

Apparently, ULTRA's Psychic Warrior's training program was turning out a lot of duds; many of the subjects becoming emotional wrecks, suicides, homicidal psychopaths, or completely insane. True, LSD enhanced the ability to Send and Receive, and even to see and hear what was miles away--but once the drug wore off, so did most of the enhanced psychic abilities.

Failure was not an option.

Project ULTRA had to quickly develop a means and find a way to mass produce an army of Psychic Warriors. National Security, the safety and future or our nation was at stake. At least, so I was told.

Months before my recruitment, The Company had found a possible solution to this vexing problem: The Company would kidnap real witches and sorcerers, and give up on the hundreds of fakes claiming to be what they're not.

The problem was finding and capturing a real sorcerer or witch, as generally they don't want to be found and resist capture--the cluster-fuck in the highlands of Vietnam illustrated exactly how difficult that can be.

This would be my first go-it-alone assignment. I was to find the brujo, don Juan Matus--the sorcerer described in Carlos Castaneda's "Yaqui Way of Knowledge."

My cover story was to be, me.

I didn't like the plan, at all. I participated in that cluster-fuck. I knew first hand what could go wrong. "Kidnapping is a bad idea," I argued. "Look what happened in Vietnam! Why not offer Castaneda's don Juan, a shit load of money?"

"Financial incentives will be offered once this man is in custody," was the answer. "Your job is to follow orders."

Fuckin' A. Bummer!

To refuse was not an option--I learned that, when assigned to the Vietnam team after my six weeks of combat training. How could I refuse now? I was in too deep, and knew too much. They'd kill me if I refused. Dead men tell no tales.

On the other hand, except for the nasty kidnapping business, the prospect of hooking up with a genuine Sorcerer, to find someone who could help me open the doors to other realities, to become a man of knowledge, to obtain cosmic wisdom, was like a dream come true.

And now, here I was, driving on a desert highway deep in the state of Sonora with not a clue as to which way to go, all because I failed to heed don Rojas' warnings. Instead, I'd fallen in love, or at least lust, with a beautiful witchy woman who done me wrong and made a mess of my first go-it-alone-assignment.

I continued to drive, cactus to the right of me, cactus to the left, then scrub, brown- then greenish- grass, a village, a town, trees then more trees... the sun slowly sinking in the west... I was on the lookout for a safe place to camp and write my field notes.

A cloud of birds flew overhead. My eyes followed. A concrete bridge and a thickening line of trees were up ahead. Beneath the bridge flowed a river. About fifty yards distant, on the right, there was a dirt road turn off disappearing into a forest of leafy green trees. Perfect!

Twenty minutes later I parked adjacent to a clearing in the woods, set up camp, sprinkled salt and piled up stones to form a circular barricade to keep out crawling critters, gathered some firewood, laid out my sleeping bag, several bottles of Coca Cola, water, my gun, log book, and a leather bag filled with seven keys to an alternate reality.

My plans for the evening? Build a fire. Practice my Yoga. Meditate. Write down everything don Rojas had said and all that transpired beginning when I first met Sophia until the moment I found myself back at the Pemex gas station. And last on my to do list: swallow the magic mushrooms, chew the peyote, and maybe smoke and eat everything else in that magic bag, and then, groove beneath the stars and, maybe, cross over into another reality.

3. Body Snatchers, Shape Shifters, Black Holes, Eaters of Souls: The Sorcerer Speaks

The sun had set and the flickering flames of the campfire were casting strange shadows upon the trees and branches which seemed to writhe and move eerily as if animated by demons within.

The darkening forest was alive with sound. Crickets chirping, owls hooting, birds singing, creatures prowling the night.

Sitting on my sleeping bag, leaning next to a tree, gun by my side, I was writing by the fire light, detailing all that had transpired, setting to words the teachings of don Rojas and everything he'd said to me as I drove us to his hacienda "while speed-reading across the pages of time;" an experience I would have dismissed as a fantastical dream if not for the brown leather bag on the floorboard of my car containing seven keys to alternate realities.

I struggled to recall all don Rojas had said during that five hour drive which seemed to have passed in five minutes, and wrote down all I could remember in the official log book as instructed by The Company.

After writing for an hour, I paused, thinking. The Company had probably sent others in pursuit of sorcerers; dozens of operatives, men like me, who received identical training and who'd gone forth to every likely sorcerer abode on this planet. That others were also searching in Mexico, or following and tracking my movements, seemed increasingly likely.

Some of the locals had said--when I returned a second or third time to their town or village--that Yankees had shown up asking questions about a long haired Gringo sporting a cowboy hat. And more than once I'd seen the same jeep going by in the opposite direction, hours after I'd turned around to go another way. Although obscured by baseball caps, the driver and passenger looked familiar.

Most likely, The Company, or the Directors of project ULTRA, didn't trust me. If my trail led them to a Sorcerer, or a Brujo, would they also kidnap and put me in a cage; or worse, kill me? Dead men tell no tales? I patted my Colt 45 affectionately. I loved this gun. It always hit exactly what I aimed at. Six weeks of hellish training paid off big time, that's for sure. Come for me and I'd take several of them with me; no doubt about it.

Truth is, I was facing a conundrum. If I located don Rojas and his ranchero, should I inform The Company? Should I let them know don Rojas even exists?

And yet, the $25,000 bounty would be enough to pay my way through college and leave me rather well off financially for the next several years. I could even buy a house!

Decisions. Decisions.

Log book in hand, I continued where I'd left off, translating from Spanish to English, and trying to quote exactly what don Rojas had said during what now seemed like a parallel time warp, a duplicate reality, paralleling yet separate from, and one day in advance of events I'd experienced today.

In the log book I wrote:

don Rojas had said "There are spirits and souls, super human espantos y fantasmas, and ghost-like beings from other realities, paralelas dimensiones, and they can be friend, indifferent, or demoníaco. There are ancestral spirits, animals spirits, terrestrial and cosmic spirits, deities, lesser gods, and greater gods, dioses mayores, who live in these other realities, and in the heavens, on other planets, extraterrestres de otros planetas! These diablos and demonios possess great power taken from the cosmic energies. This, the cosmic power is not bueno o malo, good or evil--but can be used for good and evil."

"Cosmic power? Is this the same as atomic power?" I had asked. "Or electromagnetic energy?"

don Rojas said: "Different. There is a cosmic energy, a cosmic force, energia cosmica, which is both dark and light, and forms the boundary between this, the human world, and the divine world of gods, demons, devils, diablo, demonio, espíritus y almas, and entities which live in the other dimensiones, the parallel realities. Beware the cholo of the underworld!"

"How many other realities are there?" I asked.

"Only the gods of the gods of the gods would know such things," don Rojas replied.

"Does each reality have a boundary, some kind of barrier or wall, that keeps them separate?" I asked.

"Yes, many walls, many realities, above, below, side by side," don Rojas answered. "Think of these walls as membranas, membranes with the many compartments. Like the soap bubble, Burbuja de jabón. These, the walls are porosa and poroso, porous. They have holes; agujeros negros, tiny black holes, tunnels and passageway between the parallel worlds. These walls can not be seen or touched, no se puede ver ni tocar. They are energía cósmica pura, the pure cosmic energy. Sorcerers, men of knowledge, who can see, may take, borrow, steal this energy, use the cosmic power to command and control the demonio, devils, deities, deidades, the gallinero and the beings from other dimensions, las realidades paralelas."

"How can they do that?" I asked.

"These walls," he explained, "these membranes of pure energy, are like queso Suizo, the Swiss cheese; the holes are passageways, pasajes, tunnels linking this reality with other realities and the parallel dimensions. These holes are very small, black. Pero estos agujeros son pequeños y negros. No puedes verlos. No light. Only a sorcerer may see them."

"These holes are black?" I asked.

"These holes are very small. Microscópico," don Rojas explained. "Estos agujeros son infinitamente pequeños. No color. They show no light unless they grow, become más grande. No luz brillante. Oscuridad. But these tiny holes are everywhere. All around us. Pero están en todas partes. A nuestro alrededor."

"Only a hombre de conocimiento, maestro mago, hechicero; a man of knowledge, a sorcerer who has the vision to see these holes, can see what's on the other side and open the doors to these, the other realities," don Rojas explained. "If the magician is powerful, gran poderoso, they may journey to these, the other realities, these paralelas dimensiones, and command, capture, and enslave a diablo and drag them back to this world. El demonio are sources of great power."

"And what if the demon is more powerful than the sorcerer?"

"Si, this is very dangerous. Many a sorcerer and many a bruja, has been enslaved by diablo. Si, diabolo may come willingly, he is the trickster. Sí. Verdad. ¡Así que ten cuidado! So watch out!"

"If these holes are microscopic, how can a Sorcerer, or a demon, pass through them and cross over?" I asked.

"The holes are everywhere, all around us, and may become grande, because of the cosmic energy! They grow large, they grow small. Crecen grandes, crecen pequeños. This happens all the time. When a hole grows big, grande, anyone might see it, but just for un momento because these holes quickly become small again. Infinitamente pequeño. But a true sorcerer may use secret sounds, the music of the stars and planets, música de los planetas, de las estrellas; or the Sorcerer will say, sing words a special way. Sounds, musica have cosmic energy and enlarge these holes, make them big, and a man of knowledge may call the true name of diablo who will then journey to this reality."

"How big can these holes get? Could you drive a truck through them?" I asked.

"Si! As grande as a mountain. Remember, my gringo amigo, this, the cosmic energy can be used by divine beings, seres divinos, extraterrestres de otros planetas. Si, from other planets and dimensions, de otros dimensiones. They can use this energy against humans or other divine beings to conquer, take, and gain what they desire. Tener cuidado. Beware. These entities may cross over to this world, because they are seekers of souls, alma, and wish to posses, control, enslave a human."

"They steal souls?" I asked, masking my disbelief. "What for? How's that possible?"

"The soul, el alma, is the life-force; fuerza de vida, energía vital, and has cosmic energy; a source of great power. But remember, my gringo amigo, there are many cosmic demons which live in this reality, in the heavens, on other planets, and on this world; and they too may be seekers of knowledge and eaters of souls."

"Why?"

"The power of the life force. This is why there are many wars, murders, to unleash the life force, fuerza de vida, energía vital. Diablo, the gods, can make humans loco, give them the blood lust, lujuria de sangre, and humans kill and release the life force of their victims which is eaten by demons and gods. This is why war, the fields of battle, and hospitales make for the good hunting grounds. Hospitales are especially good for stealing the souls of niños y bebés."

"They hunt children and babies? In hospitals? Why?" I asked.

"Oferta y demanda. Supply and demand," don Rojas replied. "Hospitales, they are the living graveyards where the people go to die. Many niños y bebés die in the hospitales and niños have used up little of the life force. Niños y bebés are highly prized by demons, devils, warlocks, witches, and entities from the other realities."

"Why? I don't understand."

"Stealing the souls, the life force of the healthy niños y bebés as they sleep at night, can satisfy the hunger of a single diablo," don Rojas answered. "Hospitales are the baby buffet, buffet de bebé. All you can eat!" don Rojas said with a laugh.

"This is why," don Rojas added, "brujas, witches, they steal the little ones, robar pequeños bebés. This is why so many niños y bebés die at birth or soon after."

"Wow, that's heavy," I replied, masking my disbelief.

"Demonios, devils, diablos, do not always kill the body," don Rojas replied. "Pueden poseerlo, usarlo, alimentarse de él, como un vampiro. Demonios may chose to live in the body, possess it, use it for fun, sex, to create chaos, wars, murders, evil. There is great evil in the universe, and that evil seeks human vessels, conductos to cause evil and consume the energy released from death. Evil and death unleashes great energy, power. A hombre may go loco and takes a gun and kills his familia, asesina amigos at his job, but does not know why. A mother drowns her bebes, but does not know why. They are possessed by the demonios who eat the souls of those they kill."

"So you're saying that demons can posses a normal person and make them commit murder?" I asked.

"Si. Or make them have sexuales, or get drunk, and do the bad things."

"Are demons, aliens, creatures from other realities, parallel dimensions, or other planets, are they all evil? Do they all steal bodies and souls?" I asked.

"No," he answered. "Sometimes they are only curious, like turistas de vacaciones, who wish to travel, to see strange sights, to gather knowledge, or have fun. Conocimiento, sabiduría, entretenimiento, divertirse. So, they visit this Earth, look around, eat the food, have sex, then leave."

"How can a demon posses a person?" I asked. "Does the body becomes like a puppet, or does the demon get inside the brain?

"There are many ways to posses a body," don Rojas explained. "Healthy hombres, senoritas, and babies who die, may be brought back to life by a demon; but the body remains empty, the soul is gone, vanished, so the demon they climb inside; like pouring aqua into an empty glass. The body may be possessed by entities who are good, or evil. When the soul leaves the body, another soul may enter the empty body and take over."

As explained by don Rojas: Sometimes the evil or the good entity, lives side by side with the original personality, and shares the body without the original owner realizing it. If the demon is evil, that person's entire life is cursed with bad luck and misfortune, and they bring only evil, chaos, sadness into this world, because of the diablo who lives inside them. Those possessed in this manner, may be perplexed by the bad choices they make and the bad things they do, but feel something inside them is making the choices for them.

don Rojas explained that if instead, the soul is eaten, if the healthy body suddenly dies and comes back to life, then the body may be completely possessed by that entity which may be from this universe, or a separate reality, and which acts for purposes unknown to us, or only because it wants to have fun or cause evil.

"It is very dangerous to leave the body, even during sleep, dreams," don Rojas explained. "Demonios, fantasmas, ghosts, in search of a body may take hold and break the silver thread and the human soul is cast adrift and cannot return. If the silver thread is broken, the demon can enter and take over the body."

don Rojas then stared at me and said: "The question for me, my gringo amigo, is, when you died, at age three, why did you come back to life?"

Laying aside pen and log book, I got up, stretched my legs and tossed more wood on the camp fire.

A full moon was rising over the horizon, and rays of moonshine were penetrating the dark canopy of the forest creating eerie twisting shadows of swaying, bending trees and grasping branches. The forest was alive with crickets, katydids, croaking frogs, hooting owls, and night birds singing, calling, crooning, whistling, trilling, and even shrieking like a demon or an angry cat.

Gazing longingly at my pharmacopeia of seven psychedelics, courtesy of the foresight of don Rojas, I fought the urge to immediately partake of these otherworldly delights. I was conflicted.

The field notes and log book were important. There was all night to get high. However, the magic mushrooms could take an hour to kick in. So, I stuffed a handful in my mouth, chewed the soft flesh, swallowed; then stuck a second handful in my mouth. Surprisingly, they were not unpleasant. The taste was earthy, with a slight nutty after-flavor, not different from most mushrooms.

Then, I thought, what the hell: Peyote can take an hour or more; so, I began eating the little bulbous cactus fruits by the handful. It took almost an entire bottle of Coke to get rid of the ugly bitter taste.

Next on the menu, the Ayahuasca, which is a vine and a leaf that can be eaten or mixed with hot water and swallowed like a tea or soup. I'd never tried this before, but learned all about it's properties at the Institute. Ayahuasca is very powerful magic. So, boiled some water, then down the hatch, followed by more Coca Cola to kill the extremely disgusting taste.

Despite my training at the Institute, I didn't have a clue as to what was in the remaining four satchels and decided to put off sampling these goodies, until another time.

Sitting down, ignoring the rumbling in my tummy which was protesting what'd consumed, I again began to write.

According to don Rojas, the three glowing beings, the Trinity, encountered when I died then came back to life at the tender age of three, may have been alien or intra-dimensional beings, hunters intent on capturing the life force of infants and children just before they die.

"Tell me about the demonios," don Rojas urged. "Start at the beginning, when you say you died."

"I didn't ssy they were demons," I answered. "Fact is, at first I thought the three of them were my mother, father, and aunt Mary; except they were all in white and glowing."

"Three? Glowing in white?" don Rojas interrupted. "These were not diablos," he said thoughtfully. "Again, tell me from the beginning, from the moment you died."

"Okay," I said, "If you really want to know: I was sitting on my parent's living room floor, looking at a comic book, and tossing peanuts in the air, which I caught with my mouth. A peanut went down my wind-pipe. I couldn't breath. Couldn't call out. Fell backwards onto the floor gasping for breath... and I remember, it was if I was on the ceiling staring down, and could see my father reading a newspaper, my mother stepping into the room and becoming hysterical."

"Continue," don Rojas urged.

"And then, what I remember next is: down came a concave saucer shaped structure, all lit up inside, yellow, orange, flashing lights from what looked like tiny round holes on the underside--and it was descending, enveloping my face and head... I was surrounded by men and women in white, glowing, all of them glowing, and it seemed more were arriving all the time. I remember struggling to escape, but I was strapped down."

"Where do you think you were?" don Rojas asked.

"The hospital. I think the concave-saucer-shaped thing was a gas mask for anesthesia."

"Platillo volador? With windows and all lit up like a flying saucer?" don Rojas questioned.

"Not windows--more like circular rows of light inside a bowl turned upside down. I'm sure it was for for anesthesia. Anyway, next thing I remember, I'm lying on my back, in a hospital bed in the children's ward in the hospital. This must have been after they removed the peanut from my wind pipe. I opened my eyes and three beings glowing in white were looking down at me. One of them said: 'This boy shall live,' then, next thing I know they were hovering over the hospital bed next to mine and one of the glowing beings was saying: 'this boy shall die.' And then, they were gone. Disappeared into thin air. I even climbed out of my hospital bed, and went running through the hospital looking for them. I was sure they were my parents and I couldn't understand why they left without saying goodbye or taking me with them. The nurses said I was imagining things and strapped me down so I couldn't climb out again."

"What happened to the niñito, the other little boy?" don Rojas asked.

"Died that same afternoon."

"And you also died." don Rojas asked. "Did you fly through the air when you died?"

"No. I was on the floor, choking to death, and looking down from the ceiling at the same time. I don't remember flying anywhere."

"How do you know you are the same boy who died?" don Rojas asked.

When I angrily rejected the implications of his insinuations, don Rojas expanded upon what he'd said earlier: There are demons and lost souls in search of a body. Therefore, sometimes, when young people die and the body is healthy, entities, spirits, ghosts, haints, will grab hold of the silver thread. This thread is one's life line leading from conception to death, and even to passed lives. Demons then take possession of the dead body. When the body returns to life that person's soul does not, because a demon has taken its place. The body has the same memories, but they are not the same person and have a different personality.

In my case, however, because these entities were glowing, and arrived as a Trinity, don Rojas didn't think they were hunters or demons, but may have arrived through the door to all realities, and had their own unique purpose.

The symphony of the forest had come to an abrupt halt and so did my writing I listened intently, my eyes scanning the forest, one hand reaching for the Colt 45 peaking out from the beneath my sleeping bag. The only sound was the wind gently brushing against the trees.... The silence was broken by a snapping twig, then a branch, then another: snap, crack, snap... I stood up, my gun in hand, waiting... and then the cry of an animal being eaten, a flutter of a dozen wings, and the birds, frogs, and insects again began to sing.

My stomach was churning, a bitter acid taste infiltrating my mouth--the after affects of the mushrooms, peyote and vines. But there was no vibrant psychedelic colors, no hallucinatory phantasms, no alternate realities. The drugs hadn't kicked in yet. Another Coca Cola erased the bad taste which lingered in my mouth.

Sitting down, leaning back, pen and log book in hand, I resumed writing, then hesitated. It was probably not a good idea to inform The Company of my death at age three, or the visitation of the Three Luminous Beings. Knowledge, information is power. Why give those mad scientists at the Institute any ideas about experimenting on me?

I decided, before turning them into The Company, I would remove those pages detailing my experience with the Trinity. Ignoring my stomach, I return to the writing of my field notes.

"What's the difference between a witch and a Sorcerer?" I had asked during our time-warp drive to his hacienda, in what seemed days ago, but, which had to have occurred earlier this very day in a duplicate reality.

don Rojas explained: "Snake charmers, bird-men, and those who sell potions and work magic in the street, have very little power. Brujas may have big power if they have ayudante espiritua, spirit helpers, and are assisted or have in their power the souls of animals and dead relatives, the ghosts of dead witches. Even with a spirit helper, a witch is no match for a brujo, a sorcerer."

"The most powerful brujas" don Rojas added, "are those who become the servants of powerful demonios, and diablos."

"Are all witches evil?" I asked.

"Even the good, do bad," he answered.

As told to me by don Rojos: Brujas: Witches are almost always women and even the good witches cause much evil. They may use their power to sicken or kill the people they like or love, a consequence of the irrational nature of a woman's mind and her sensitive nature. When a woman gets mad, she may go "loco," he said.

According to don Rojas: "Some witches work magic, both good and evil, in their sleep. As they dream, their spirits leave their bodies and may attack sleeping neighbors and those they hate or love."

"Some bad witches and their demonio masters crave human blood and the flesh of virgins and beautiful young women, children and babies," he said. "These brjuas are vampiras. Sorcerers only use sangre for hechizos magicos, casting spells. Witches may sacrifice babies, virgins, and men, to please or gain help from a demonio. A sorcerer would not do this."

"Can witches fly?" I asked.

"A flying brjua," don Rojas answered, "is almost always a female demonio, and not a bruja at all; unless she has a powerful spirit helper, ayudante espiritua, or becomes the slave of a powerful diablo and has a lesser demonio in her power. A powerful demon can call upon brujas, who will appear at the demon's command."

"Witches flying on broomsticks is a myth?" I asked.

"Si. Brujas are very social. They love to travel, visit, have parties, gossip, share magic recipes, and gather together day or night. La brujería! But brooms they use only to clean the floor."

"Why all the visiting?"

"To talk, gossip, share spells and recipes, admire new clothes, and to worship diablo or a powerful demon who has enslaved them. At night, por la noche, when they gather, they remove their clothes. Dance naked; wild crazy dances, a sexual frenzy, frenesí obsceno, and have sex, relaciones carnales, lesbianas, with each other, with animals and diablos, and men they bewitch then kill. La brujería! A woman's naked body, her sex has great power and can attract the attention of demonios, fantasma, and spirits who may join in the orgía and bestow great power. A naked female, her body has mucho power."

"Can a witch visit another dimension, or cross over to another reality?" I asked.

"Si, if she is the slave of a demon," he answered. "But beware, pero cuidado, the female demonios who dwell in the other realities; they are like queens, reinas princesas, and rule over kingdoms where dwell demons and devils. They may cross over to this reality, and they are very dangerous."

"How are they dangerous?"

don Rojas answered: "Demons, devils, are tricksters. Woman is expert at creating illusions, making a man desire her even when the body and face is old and ugly. All women know this, which is why they use the makeup, the perfume, to trick the man."

"Are witches always ugly?" I asked.

"Witches and female demons can be very beautiful, but this is often an illusion," don Rojas cautioned. "The female demon uses sex and beauty like a weapon, a knife to stick in your heart to suck your blood and eat your soul. The female can use magic and make the man go crazy with lust, women too. But beware, a male demon may cast a spell to make him look like the beautiful woman. These demons feast upon men, and the women. Once you yield to her embrace, diablo will enslave your body and soul. She may put you in a cage, imprison you in a hole in the ground. Your life becomes a living hell."

"Demons are shape shifters?" I asked.

"Si."

"Is it true that shape shifters can take the form of animals, such as birds?" I asked.

"Si, that is correct. Birds, four legged animals, other humans," he answered.

"And you take the shape of an eagle?" I asked.

don Rojas ignored my question.

"Why take the shape of a bird? Why not just fly to wherever you want to go, instantly, in spirit form, and then take human shape when you get there?" I asked.

According to do Rojas: To travel as a spirit is dangerous and the trajectory of the flight is very difficult to control. Freed of the body, the soul may forget its personal identity and where it wants to go and why. In consequence, it may also lose navigational control, become easily distracted and travel wherever a new whim directs it.

The body also becomes an empty vessel, he said, A tempting target to become possessed by a demon who takes hold of the silver thread, and who may refuse to let you back in, transforming you into a disembodied spirit, a ghost, that is neither dead or alive, but wonders the earth lost and confused.

According to do Rojas: Shape shifting is the transformation of the Sorcerer's body, into another body, and therefore the body is never an empty vessel.

"So, it's safer to shape-shift and become a bird?" I asked.

"Or drive," don Rojas said laughing. "Or take a plane," he added, slapping his thigh and laughing out loud. "But here in the desert, in this country," he added becoming serious. "flying as a bird or an eagle can be much faster. There are very few good roads."

"But how is it possible to change the body into something else?" I asked.

don Rojas replied: "The child he looks like the mother and father, Si? The humans they come from the apes, evolution, Si? The humans and the apes they look similar, Si?"

"Yes," I replied. "But what's that got to do with shape-shifting?"

"The evolution, humans from apes, apes from the monkeys, where did it all begin? Only the gods know this," he said. "But long ago, humans must have come from the lizards and the birds and the fish. These animals, they are like the parents."

"Sorry, I don't get it," I said.

don Rojas' said in reply: "Evolución! The genes, the DNA, all inherited, from the beginning, and still in the body! Inherited. In the cells. But the DNA of the bird, fish, snake, is sleeping inside your cells. The Sorcerer, a man of great power, can use the energy to awaken the DNA of the fish, the bird, the wolf, that sleeps in the cells. The body of the Sorcerer can then become the fish, the bird, or the wolf by concentrating the mind's eye."

"Why not just project your mind to where you want to go, and stay home in your body?" I asked.

"Because the demons may cut the silver thread and steal the body," he answered. "Only a sorcerer of great power, would take such a risk."

"How does smoking and eating special plants, or drinking these magic brews, give power?" I asked. "I know certain drugs, like LSD, can enhance the senses, expand consciousness, but how do they create power? How is this different from cosmic power?"

"The power is in the brain," don Rojas said, pointing to his head. "The brain cells gives power to the mind. The brain cell, every célula in the body, has enough energy to destroy a city."

"Like an atomic bomb?" I asked.

"Si! The atoms in the brain cells, they have great power, the cosmic energy. A Tetlachihuic can focus the mind and release that great energy, which is power!" he said with a flourish.

"If the power is already there, and you can focus to release it, then why take mushrooms or peyote?" I asked.

don Rojas explained: "El cerebro no quiere ver. The brain, it does not want to see too much. See too much, and go loco! The brain it closes the door and the windows, so not see too much. The power is there, but the brain does not know how to open the door, because the door is hidden. "

"How can the brain see too much?"I asked.

"Do you want to taste the sky or the dirt beneath your feet?" he asked. "Do you wish to hear the thoughts of animals and plants when you lay down to sleep? Do you wish to see ghosts and demons when you sit down to eat? The brain closes these doors and windows so you do not go loco!"

"Teonanácatl, the flesh of the gods, and Mescalito, the food of the gods, can open the doors and the windows, and release the energy, "don Rojas' explained. "The lighting a match to explode a bomb; a small explosion makes a big explosion and releases, from tiny atoms, from the cells in the brain, tremendous power. Release that power with the help of Teonanácatl, Mescalito, and other magical plants, then the other realities, the parallel dimensions, will open up, right before your eyes."

I stopped writing. I'd lit the fuse of not one, but three of the ingredients from don Rojas's magical leather sack; and they were beginning to kick in and explode away the doors and windows to these alternate realities... I was hallucinating. And what I seeing, was blowing my mind!

4. Season of the Witch: The Demon Princess Queen

The three keys from don Rojas' magic bag of psychedelics, I'd ingested, had not yet opened the doors to any separate realities. However, the key was in the lock, the handle was turning, and the first light from the other side was beginning to trickle in, effecting and distorting my perceptions of this reality.

As Grace Slick, of Jefferson Airplane, in 1967 sang: "One pill makes you large. And one pill makes you small. And the ones that mother gives you don't do anything at all, Go ask Alice, when she's ten feet tall. And if you go chasing rabbits, and you know you're going to fall, tell 'em a hookah smoking caterpillar has given you the call, to call Alice, when she was just small. When the men on the chessboard get up and tell you where to go, and you've just had some kind of mushroom, and your mind is moving slow, go ask Alice, I think she will know. When logic and proportion have fallen sloppy dead. And the white knight is talking backwards. And the red queen's off with her head. Remember what the dormouse said: Feed your head, feed your head."

don Rojas had explained, to open those doors to parallel realities requires an unlocking of the perceptual senses, to free the mind to see what is right before the eyes, instead of forcing reality to conform to expectations. Perceptual distortions are followed by hallucinations as one opens the doors and peers through the windows leading to the other side. To open and step through those doors requires courage and an opening of the mind which must expand to take in and perceive what's on the other side.

The mushrooms, peyote, Ayahuasca, I'd ingested, were finally beginning to kick in those doors of perception. The log book was shrinking, becoming far away, like I was far up in the tree branches looking down from a distance. Suddenly the pen and log book loomed up in size, as if I had grown smaller, the words on the page becoming huge, the letters twitching, squirming, and my normally terrible handwriting became elegant with swirls and curly cues which were flowing across the page. I could taste the sweet and sour flavor of the paper, and the ink which was bitter, acidy, metallic, disgusting.

I swallowed and washed my mouth with Coca Cola which became a wiggling-liquid-rope-like snake stretching down my throat into my stomach. I tried to cough it up, spitting coke from my mouth and nose which splattered, turning into little crawling fluorescent worms and neon snakes.

Nauseous, my stomach was in twisting turmoil, cramping, churning, expanding in two directions, making me feel a need to vomit and take a gigantic shit at the same time. I struggled to my feet. My hand and arm passed completely through the center of the tree as if made not of wood but mush. My body, head, and neck stretched like rubber and coiled around the tree, as I attempted to look at my hand sticking out the other side.

Trees, bark, branches, leaves, were in motion, agitated by an inner restlessness, looming large, then small, shedding tiny spinning molecules which formed small colorful neon clouds which twinkled as they floated away.

Dizzy, my stomach in knots, I upchucked and vomited, then more vomitus, my entire stomach and intestines rising up through my throat, erupting from my mouth, splattering the ferns, moss, leaves, twigs and broken branches which made up the forest floor--all of which became alive with sparks and a kaleidoscope of colors. And from the morass of vomitus, crawled multi-colored fluorescent worms, centipedes, spiders, mice, rats, and creepy crawling things which sprouted wings and flew away.

I collapsed back into a sitting position against the tree, dazzled now by a rainbow of colors, and sparkling lights. Plucking hold of a brightly lit amber leaf, I could taste the green-color through my finger tips! It was pulsating, radiating visible colors of energy. I could feel its life-force flow between my fingers. And then, I could see the individual cells of the leaf; and then the fine cellular microstructure became magnified, its little veins and the surrounding cells pulsating with life. It was all very real-- as if my eyes had become a microscope.

And then the leaf began to fractionate into billions of square-shaped particles, disintegrating and becoming a cloud of atoms and molecules emitting an orchestra of sound, each individual note becoming optical as it floated away.

Every sound of the forest, the wind in the trees, frogs croaking, birds singing, became an optical image, exploding in fountains of color and forming ripples upon a rainbow sea of air. Floating among the trees and above the camp fire were multi-colored geometric patterns, spirals, circles, funnels, whirlpools, arabesques rearranging themselves in constant flux, bouncing and ricocheting against one another, against the ground, and bouncing among the branches of the trees.

A green snake crawled out of a spiraling arabesque which lay pulsating on the ground near the camp fire. The creature's green eyes were luminous, the body flashing neon, skin squirming and radiating sparks of light. The snake sprouted four legs, became a lizard and walked over to one of the four unused satchels and gave it a sniff.

Looking back up at me, the lizard said: "You should smoke this one next."

I erupted in laughter. Each laugh creating a physical-optical presence, like an oscilloscope, the waves of each laugh moving through the air forming whirl-pools and arabesques.

The lizard crawled up on my left boot, then up my leg, stopping at my knee. It changed colors, became fluorescent, and grew round spots which levitated above its body.

"What's so funny?" the lizard asked.

"A talking lizard. Wow! Far fucking out!" Again, I erupted in uncontrolled laughter, which echoed through the forest as if transmitted by an array of giant loudspeakers in a football stadium.

"Echo!" I said aloud, and yes, I could hear and see the spiraling "Echo echo echo" booming through the forest.

The lizard skittered back toward the satchels, grabbed it with its mouth and arm, then dragged it toward me. Behind the lizard were a train of dozens of ghost-like lizards, overlapping, one behind the other, as if I was observing duplicates in parallel dimensions, each slightly out-of-phase with the other, only to merge with the lizard when it stopped near my hand.

The lizard dropped the little leather bag near my fingers. The satchel was twitching, animated, as if alive.

"You should smoke this," the lizard said.

"Why?" I asked.

The lizard doubled in size, became crimson, then emerald, then scarlet and then grew glowing multi-colored stripes which circled over and under its body. An additional pair of human-like fingers and arms sprouted from its body, and it placed the satchel in my hand.

The lizard said: "Smoke this, and the doors to other realities will open."

I reached for the bone pipe but became mesmerized by the sparks of light and multiple arm-hand trails my arm left in its wake. I waved my hand creating a ka-leidoscope of ghost-like-arm-hand-trails of multiple ghost-like hands; and then, took a closer look: I could see the cellular structure of my skin, the tiny cells on the palm of my hand; it was if my eyes had become a tunneling microscope, probing beneath the layers. I was reminded of the first time I'd taken LSD. There were sweat glands and layers of cells which were swallowing up little particles of grit, and below them, column-shaped cells which were also in motion, pushing toward the surface. I could see the cell membranes, cytoplasm, nuclei. My eyes continued to tunnel: tendons, muscles, bones, blood vessels inside of which were red and white cells flowing in a sea of red plasma--forward then slightly back, then further forward, then slightly back in rhythm to the beating of my heart... and my eyes continued to tunnel, until I could see completely through my hand; and there was the fluorescent, glowing, green-yellow-red lizard holding up the little leather satchel of magic.

I took the satchel and it began squirming, wiggling, like a little animal; then opening and closing, becoming a multi-finger fist, then a blooming flower, a pul-sating vagina, and finally a toothless mouth with sucking lips which sighed with pleasure.

"Smoke me," it said, so I did.

First one puff, then another... the shimmering lizard watching, growing larger, sprouting a spiked tail, the extra legs becoming flapping multi-jointed wings. Its grotesque body silhouetted by the camp fire, the creature looked evil, dangerous. Upward it flew, round and round the fire, dozens of ghostly overlapping lizards trailing in its wake... Tongues of flame each of which became dancing, leaping sprites and homunculi rose up above the camp fire, circling and paying homage to the flying lizard king.

There was an orchestra of sound and light, the trees twisting, swaying to the music of the forest, waving their branches like so many multi-jointed elongated arms and fingers... and then, metamorphosis, trees transformed, taking humans shapes, stepping into the clearing, wearing ponchos and sombreros, circling the camp fire, now dancing, playing flutes, oboes, clarinets, tambourines, stripping off their hats and clothes, becoming beautiful naked women of every flavor and color: Reds, Blacks, Whites, Orientals, Arabs, Spaniards, Indians, Persians, Islanders from the Seven Seas, singing, dancing, sinuous, undulating, writhing, bending, twisting, pumping, grinding, gyrating, swaying breasts and buttocks, and beckoning with open arms and lips: come-to-me...come-to-me...

The lizard, now a flying crimson dragon dived in and out of the camp fire flames. Combustion! It was burning, on fire, trailing flames, turning black, then shrinking to a puff of smoke which was sucked into a tiny oval black hole of nothingness. Poof!

Like the clicking of an off switch, all sound, singing, dancing, and movement stopped; the symphony of the forest and music of the naked maidens replaced by silence punctuated by the distant footsteps of a spotted jaguar which emerged from between the trees in a menacing crouch. I was coming closer, stalking, snarling, salivating, staring at me with hungry, devouring, green luminous predatory eyes over the flames of the dancing fire.

My body was suddenly imprisoned by the branches of the tree which became enveloping arms and hands, holding me tight, unmoving.

And with a roar the spotted jaguar leaped up and over the flames, open mouthed, baring fangs and claws and exploding in an arc of millions of multi-colored fractals, tiny six-pointed stars, squares, triangles; each disintegrating into a kaleidoscopic cloud of molecules which drifted outward and upward, coalescing, becoming multi-colored butterflies, which became the glowing eyes of fantastical beasts that stepped out of the darkness, forming an outer circle surrounding the inner circle of divine, lusty, beautiful naked women.

The singing dancing playing of musical instruments erupted in a wild writhing frenzy... the inner circle of beautiful naked women singing, whirling, prancing, clockwise; and, in the outer circle, counterclockwise, fantastical beasts, monstrosities, and grotesque assemblages of distorted and mismatched body parts resembling part goat, rabbit, cat, pig, reptile, snake, frog, bat, rat, and with barbed tails, and multiple eyes, hands, claws, flippers, horns, and sagging distended breasts growing where they were never meant to be.

And from the forest emerged ghastly, decrepit old women with ancient wrinkled skin, flat distended breasts, holding torches and followed by a procession of cats...and at the lead, a crone as old as death, her eyes clouded over with muck. And they too joined the outer circle of dancing monstrous beasts.

As they sang, danced, screeched, chanted, and screamed, a tiny black dot, which became a small bubble appeared above the camp fire, hovering, then expanding, illuminated within by a sparkling rainbow of cadmium, carmine, amber, emerald, and violet light.

As this kaleidoscopic bubble of light ballooned outward, the external forest, my surroundings, began to pixelate, forming cracks and fissures, becoming like pieces of a puzzle being pushed apart, all of which fell outward, collapsing sideways-- the fabric of this reality toppling like a house of cards by the expanding concave arc of multi-colored flames of light.

The music, singing, dancing stopped. The naked, nubile beauties, dropped to their knees, facing the gigantic concave circle of light, their arms and hands waving, gesticulating above their heads in hosanna adoration and supplication. The outer circle of monstrosities and old toothless naked women were bowing worshipfully.

Two giant antelope-horned rabbits hopped forward from within the outskirts of the far right and left half of this now panoramic concave bubble of prismatic fiery light. They stood up at attention, clapped their front paws together. There was an explosion of flaming, blazing, incandescent, brilliant color...revealing a heavenly hell within.

I was gazing into an alternate reality which had appeared right before my eyes.

It was as if a veil had been ripped away to the left and to the right of this reality revealing a parallel world on the other side.

The concave formation was titanic, panoramic, curving above, below, and almost all around me, forming a circular curvature of vast proportions, and revealing within: sky, clouds, landscape which mirrored those of our world, but of pulsating hues and colors distinctly alien to our own. Purple clouds, a sky of gold, grass of blue, bejeweled fruiting trees and blossoming flowers of every hue of the rainbow, and all illuminated within by pulsating, living, inner lights.

The two giant antelope-horned rabbits clapped their paws and the interior landscape fractionated, pixelated, shattered and fell, revealing the interior of a golden colonnaded temple and impossibly lovely, scantily clad, angelic yet sensuous women adorned with flashing jewels, silks, furs, and revealing clothes of heavenly design; all lounging, sitting, or lying upon richly textured divans and cushions of silver, platinum, gold; and admiring each other or gazing lovingly at their own reflections in golden mirrors of light.

And their hair and all that these alluring beauties wore was in a continual whimsical feminine-flux of changing style, color, and cut. Shoes, makeup, eyeshadow, bracelets, necklaces, rings, pendants, chokers, bangles, cuffs were in a frenzy of becoming this or transformed into that--and all it took was a wave of a delicate hand or an enticing graceful touch.

Two legged lioness, tigresses, and all manner of female cats with faces and heads of lovely ladies, and those with the heads of felines but with naked female-human bodies, strutted about on high heels, playing flutes, strumming stringed instruments, cooling the air with feathered fans, or carrying golden trays laden with jewels, fruit, meats, and diamond studded golden chalices of drink. Winged angelic cherubic babies flittered through the air, happy, singing and playing golden harps.

There were no men I could see. Instead, guarding this heaven of feminine delights, were bull dogs and black mastiffs but with heads of bearded men immobilized by chains embedded in the flooring attached to jeweled metal collars locked tightly around their necks. The dog-men sat on their rumps, quiet, obedient, alert, watching all.

And standing at the center, a breathtakingly alluring, gloriously and sublimely lovely, enticingly sexy long-legged beauty who could only be a princess of the realm, or its queen. Her nails were long, painted in glowing vibrant colors that changed by the moment, her hair black, then red, then blue, then gold, a continual flux of styles and cuts. She stood on six-inch spiked heels and was draped in folds of richly embroidered silk, and an opaque, nearly see-through gossamer golden gown which hid as much it revealed.

The princess queen's diamond eyes were upon me; an inviting come-to-me, innocently devilish smile on her lovely lips. With a slight swing of her hips, she took a step forward, then another, her gossamer gown revealing long legs and a shaved paradise up above.

I had no idea if this was an alternate reality, a parallel dimension, or an incredibly realistic hallucination, but was enjoying myself immensely.

And to my right and left, the naked nubile beauties and the monsters and toothless old women, formed a two tier gauntlet, a passageway to the pulsating circle of this heavenly alternate reality of female sexuality. Those of the gauntlet were bowing and chanting, their hands together as if in prayer.

"Come to me," said the princess queen, in a voice both music and honey. She beckoned with fingers ringed with sapphires, rubies, diamonds, gold.

All the women in both realities began singing, "Love her, take her, love her, take her..."

With a swing of her hips, the princess queen took another step, her golden gown swishing aside revealing long legs and heaven above. "Come to me, my handsome man," she purred in a voice hypnotic and promising a sensuous paradise of otherworldly delights.

She put fingers to kissing lips, and gazing at me with innocent eyes, slipped a finger inside her mouth, sucking, in and out.

Fuckin A!

The two-legged cat women, in this alternate reality, were strolling forward, holding silver treasure chests in their paws, which they set on the floor, then opened, revealing gold, diamonds, rubies; as if these precious jewels and metals were now mine to own.

All the impossibly lovely women within this other worldly tableau, had removed their clothes and stood, kneeled, or lay naked with legs spread, sensuously humping, grinding, and showing all as they sang: "Love her, take her, love her, take her..."

Holy mother of god! Hallucination or not, I wanted to fuck them all!

I'd grown a hard-on as big as a rocket, and was on my feet, stepping forward between the gauntlet and rows of beautifully naked nymphs and grotesque monsters and ugly old women.

"Love her, take her, love her, take her..." they sang.

Hips swaying, succulent breasts inviting, the princess queen took another step forward, a finger slowly slipping in and out of her sucking mouth, the other hand rubbing lewdly, obscenely exploring between her golden thighs.

"Come to me," she said, her voice mesmerizing, intoxicating, hypnotic and innocently sweet.

Midway between the gauntlet, just yards away from the Princess Queen and her heaven of pussy galore, I stopped. Two emotions, conflicting thoughts raged through my brain and battled for the supremacy of my mind: Fuck her brains out - Run for your life! Fuck her brains out - Run for your life!

Two more steps forward, I again came to a halt before this portal to an undulating unreality. No, this is crazy. I'm not going in there. I might never come back. Might end up with a dog's body, chained to the floor. Or worse.

"Love her, take her, love her, take her..." they sang. But the women and monsters forming the gauntlet, were pushing, shoving me forward, their voices becoming harsh, angry, insistent.

The giant antelope-horned rabbits clapped their hands and which rang like thunder. My eyes grew wide with horror. The sky was darkening; crimson clouds in flames; lightning flashing; the hounds from hell straining at their chains howling, snarling, growling; cat-women backs arching baring fangs and claws, hissing, yowling; overturned golden dishes, bloody pieces of hands, arms, eyeballs scattered, and fallen goblets of blood splattered; cherubs now devils transformed into flying snapping fanged jaws and gaping mouths...fires raged, smoke billowed... The heavenly realm of the Princess Queen had turned into a raging hell.

The sky was burning, flames licking the ground, setting clouds and trees aflame. The ground was saturated with pools of blood, from which crawled loathsome vermin. In the far distance behind the temple, there were caverns and pits of torture, pitiful screams and cries echoing deep from within... and from the pits emerged fiery winged daemons with coiled barbed tails and horns thrusting from their heads, carrying before them men and women impaled on stakes like banners, flags and trophies of war ... one of whom looked like me, bleeding, tortured and nailed to a cross which they carried forth...

The princess queen stood waiting in the midst of this nightmare reality, her beautiful face malevolent, radiating evil, and lust.

I tried to step back, turn around. They surrounded me: the naked beauties, monstrosities, and the hideously ugly old crones, all pushing, shoving, hissing, snarling. I tried to fight back. To break loose. They were too many. Dozens of hands had taken hold, grabbing my arms, neck, and hair, violently pushing, shoving, dragging me toward that hellish reality, my ears now ringing with curses, screeches, howls, and the nightmarish laughter of these harpies from hell.

"Bring him to me!" The princess queen commanded.

The beauties and uglies were tearing at my clothes, scratching, biting, dragging, pulling. Dozens of arms and hands lifting me up, carrying me forward, on my back, facing upward, helpless, closer, closer to the gates of that darkening fire-breathing demon-haunted hell.

"Die die die..." they screeched.

And far above me, a black creature circling, wings spread, now wings folded, soaring down from the sky, a living rocket aimed right at my head.

A crow as black as night, clutching two small leather satchels, slammed into my chest and took hold. Cocking its head, eyes upon me, it looked to the left then the right taking in the nightmarish scene; then with a spreading of wings, transformation: an old but beautiful woman straddled my waist and chest, her legs wrapped around me tight. From a satchel in her right hand she placed a cookie-like substance between her lips, and from a satchel in her left tossed a red powder into the air which became dazzling, polychromatic, incandescent, phosphorescence glittering, shimmering, flaming stars and particles of light.

And then: No longer a crow, but metamorphosis: eyes of fire, face of desire, lips like the sun.

Sophia?

Mouthing oaths, curses, and incantation, Sophia began waving two black feathered fans each emitting tongues of blinding light.

I was dropped to the ground.

As glittering, shimmering, twinkling cloud of dust began to fall, the old crones screamed curses, and then they, and their cats, turned and ran, disappearing into the forest and the darkness of night.

The nubile beauties stepped back, back, fear marring their lovely faces, and then, they froze, their hands and arms now branches, bodies becoming trees; the monstrosities melting, erupting into flames, becoming puffs of smoke which a sudden wind blew away.

Spinning round Sophia faced the demon princess queen who ruled that hellish parallel dimension of lust and obscene. The two women gazed upon the other's beauty, up and down, hair, skin, makeup, jewels, legs, shoes...lionesses appraising steak.

Laughing, the princess queen created a circle of crimson-amber-scarlet fire with a wave of her arms and hands, and the bubble of light that formed that other reality, imploded, growing smaller, becoming a black hole that disappeared from sight.

Stunned, shocked, my heart was racing in fright. What the hell had happened? I looked all around me. Trees were trees, my campfire burning bright, only the trampled vegetation was proof of what transpired that night.

I gazed at Sophia with shock and stunned relief.

Her back toward me, I called her name.

"Sophia? How'd you do that? What were those things? What the hell just happened? How you get here? What was that place? Was that fucking real?

She stiffened her back and shoulders and ignored me.

"Sophia! You just save my life! Fuckin A. Those things were going to kill me!"

Sophia turned abruptly, strode forward, her face full of anger.

"Bastardo! Es esto lo que buscas? Sueñas con putas," she hissed, waving her hand over her shoulder, behind her at what had been an alternate reality but was no more: "Putas! Putas! This is what you wish for?"

Sophia slapped me hard and yelled: "You are a child, a fool who will never learn to see. Go back to your America, stupid Yankee gringo man."

I ignored the slap, and opened my arms, a smile upon my scratched and bloodied face.

"Sophia, I am so happy to see you... I...I've been searching for you... I have so many questions. and...but, looking at you makes my heart sing!"

She was snarling, enraged, and with a shove pushed me away. "All you think of is putas, gringo man. Evil follows you! We do not want you here. Go home. Go away."

"But, Sophia, I... don't know what you're talking about. Those things, those women, I was trying to escape."

"You conjured them. Its what your heart desires. Sex with Putas. You are a whore. Now go away," she answered angrily.

"I...don't understand why you're mad at me. I... didn't conjure, I... well, a snake... a snake that became a lizard told me to..."

"A snake? A lizard!" she hissed. "You obeyed a snake? Stupid Gringo. You are loco!"

"I thought it was a spirit helper," I replied.

"A spirit helper from hell," she answered. "Putas from hell are your spirit helpers. This is what you want. Putas. Whores."

"Listen. That's not true. I miss you. I've been searching for you..."

"Why?" Sophia demanded.

"I really care about you... that night we were together... There was something special between us."

"Yes, your dick," she snarled. "And it is not so special."

"Sophia... I... think... I love you!" Oh shit! I thought: Big mistake. Never never never tell a woman you love her!

Her face softened, her questioning eyes searching my face. So, I said it again.

Stepping closer, I took her hands in mine. "Yes, I think I love you, Sophia."

Jerking her hands free, she stepped away: "How can you love me? You do not know me? You are a stupid child," she said.

"Sophia," I said, imploring, "But I do love you."

"Lust," she said dismissively. "Sex is not love."

And, truth is, I did love her. I was bewitched by her beauty: loved her face, her skin, her scent, her body... and the way she made love. Even her personality! She was a bitch, but she had inner beauty! And now she saved my life. She must care about me!

"Honestly, I feel as if I've waited my entire life for you!" I said.

She scoffed: "Your entire life? You are a baby. What do you know of love, of life?"

"I know I can't stop thinking about you. And, you must care about me. When we were together, making love, we were so close, two hearts beating as one."

Sophia scoffed. "It was just sex. Meant nothing."

"Then why are you here? Why'd you save me from those, demons? That creature from hell?

"My father sent me," she answered. "A daughter must honor her father's wishes."

"You must care about me!" I insisted.

"No. I hate you. Go away."

Again I took her hands in mine. "Admit it. You do care about me."

"No. I don't," she insisted, but, she didn't pull away.

"Admit it!"

"Maybe a little," she replied.

Leaning close, I tried to kiss her, but she gently pushed me back.

"Your face is bloodied. You are hurt," she said, opening her blouse, giving me a glimpse of her perfectly luscious breasts. She removed one of three satchels hanging by a leather strap from her neck.

"Lay down," she said. "let me take care of your wounds."

And she did. Mixing the ingredients from her satchel with water and her saliva, and tearing away fabric from my already ruined shirt, she gently applied this magic healing elixir to my chest, arms, and hands.

"I do love you, Sophia!"

"Hush," she replied, and leaning close she tended to the cuts and scratches on my face, her lips close to my own.

Throwing my arms around her, my lips met hers, and we kissed passionately, holding each other close, her tongue playing with mine.

"Sophia... I do love you..." I murmured, kissing her lips, throat, breasts. "I want to be with you, to love you."

"Banámichi...Then you must follow the heart," she purred, and kissed my lips, face, eyes...

"Follow the heart..." she repeated softly, then pressed her tender lips next to mine...

...I felt sleepy, tired, exhausted...

Silence!

Opening my tired eyes I gazed through the dusty windshield at a big black crow standing on the hood of my car. It cocked its head to the left and right staring at me as I stared back.

I caught my reflection in the rear view mirror. My face and neck were scratched, bruised, shirt ripped and torn.

I looked around. I was back at the Pemex gas station. A short, fat sweating woman and two dirty, squirming brats stood in a dilapidated doorway. A tall thin Mexican man was striding toward my car, a dirty rag in his hands.

Fuckin A. It was deja vu all over again.

And then, with a girlish-human-like cackle, the crow laughed, flapped its wings, and was gone.

5. Warriors: Killing Devils and Demons

Deja vu again!?? I was stunned. Shocked. Exhausted. And my face looked like warmed over shit!

I tried to think, reason out what happened; but it was all a swirling confusion.

What was real, what was not? Sophia? don Rojas? The demoness goddess from hell? Have I been sitting here the entire time in a dream state and hallucinating? Am I a victim of a project ULTRA mind-control experiment?

The scratches, bruises, bites, although healing, looked real. They certainly felt real!

Opening the glove box, retrieving the field notebook, I began reading: it was all there, all my notes, everything I'd written up to the moment I began vomiting at the campsite. And, yes, there was the brown sack, lying on the floor boards; four satchels empty of contents!

Fucking A!

Twisting round, checking the surroundings: yes, everything was the same: fat woman in the doorway with her kids, two old men sitting in the shade.

The tall skinny Mexican stood next to driver's side of my car, looking down, asking if I wanted gas? So, everything was not exactly the same. The first time I met the owner outside the car. And, I certainly didn't have bites on my body! But I sure did now! Hope those witch-bitches didn't give me rabies! And, goddamn it, this was my favorite shirt and now it's all ripped and torn to hell!

Fucking A!

A few minutes later, I exited the cantina, feeling totally refreshed, like a new man.

Studying the map, I traced the route I'd already taken along highway 14. The name of a city, located off highway 89, caught my eye: "Banámichi? Where'd I hear that before?"

Retrieving a visitor's atlas from the glove box, and looking up Banámichi, I read: "The heart of the Rio Sonoro River Valley."

"Follow the heart," she'd said.

Sophia!

I sat in the car thinking: Why did she keep sending me here? Back to this same time and place? Or were these parallel realities, the same time, but a different reality? I couldn't figure out why she was doing this to me. don Rojas said a sorcerer could change the past. Was Sophia trying to change the past? Make me start the day all over and do something different? Maybe she was trying to guide me, give me another chance to find the way to the hacienda? Or did she want me to give up and go home? Then why give me a hint where to find her? Just to steal energy from me? No. Sophia must like me, a lot! What the hell was she up to? Why?

Who can understand the mind of a woman?

I looked at the map: Banámichi,

Fuckin A! I was on my way.

But first: detail all that I'd experienced after I began vomiting back at the camp site, and to do it now before fading from memory. So, I drove my VW to the shady side of the cantina, and sipping Coca Cola, began to write.

About 20 minutes later a black jeep drove by--the same jeep I'd seen several times since beginning this adventure three weeks ago. Before, I'd only had a glimpse of the driver and passenger whose faces were obscured by baseball caps. Now I caught a full facial view of the skin-head sitting ramrod straight, riding shot-gun: Snake Eyes! The same SOB who made my life miserable for six hellish weeks of training in combat and urban and jungle warfare, shooting at pop-up targets of Fidel Castro, Hitler, Karl Marx, Stalin, Nikita Khrushchev, Che Guevara, Chairman Mao, and Ho Chi Minh. There followed another week in a sweltering mountainous Vietnamese jungle which led to a massive clusterfuck. What a bummer.

Here's the background:

After I reached an agreement with The Company and General Wheeler's men, military doctors determined I was legally blind, and they classified me "4-F." No military draft and no Vietnam for me: LA LA LA, HA HA HA. Then came the big surprise. I was going to receive special forces military training.

"Why?" I demanded. "That was not part of the deal!"

That's when they explained the deal: They were going to send me to some very dangerous parts of the world; North Korea, Siberia, and countries I'd never heard of; sometimes as part of a team or as a go-it-alone operative. I had to receive proper military training.

I was told: "You will receive special forces training. We are not going to transport you into a potential combat zone or into an area overrun with bandits, rebels, warriors, or crazed tribesmen, only to have you come back in a body bag, your mission a failure, enemies alerted, and all the money and effort put into your training a complete waste of government expenditures. This is for your protection and ours. You will be properly trained and you will obey or suffer the consequences of insubordination."

Although I'd had no military training, I was transported to a special forces military camp in North Carolina with my orders and long hair; both of which immediately pissed off the Colonel who ran the show. Nor was I welcomed with open arms by Lt. Snake Eyes, the sergeants, or the skin-heads each of whom were veterans--many with kills on their resumes. These bad asses were the super elite, who, out of hundreds had been selected for this unique three month course, seven weeks of which were to be my personal hell.

The hell began the first day with module 1: basic combat training. For everyone else, module 1 was to be a seven week course followed by another three months in more advanced modules. But my training was limited to and came to an end on the sixth week. As to the cross cultural instructional phase, well, surprise: I spent a week in the highlands of Vietnam.

The first morning began with a long lecture by the Colonel as he stood ramrod straight, stern, unsmiling, boots and helmet shining, all spit and polish. He was old, at least 60, graying, having served as a LT during WWII, in the 45th Division of the Seventh Army, fighting at Palermo and Messina under General George Patton; and when that war ended transferring between services and becoming a Special Forces Marine, rising to the rank of Major during the Korean War, then, in Vietnam, promoted to Lt Colonel where he commanded a regiment of six brigades.

He had a swashbuckling personality. Dashing, fearless, courageous, and rumored to be unstable; recklessly putting his own life and that of his men at unnecessary risk all in the pursuit of glory. His reckless, fearless quest for honor and glory finally led to the loss of his command, coupled with a promotion and assignment here at this training facility as a full fledged Colonel.

He ordered us to take notes, standing, in the sun, not sitting down because: "I don't want a bunch of waffle asses in this unit. These lectures, the lessons you learn, will do you the most good standing on your feet, because its on your feet and not sitting on your ass, that you will be doing the killing."

"Make no mistake about it. This is what your training is all about: War means fighting. Fighting means killing. Your job? Find the enemy, attack him, kill him."

"You will learn self-confidence. Centuries ago, Shakespeare wrote, Our doubts are traitors, and make us lose the good we oft might win, by fearing to attempt."

"Doubt is a liar. Never make friends with doubt. You are not beaten until you admit it. Don't ever! Doubt will lose battles and kill you and your men. Take the initiative. Initiative won't kill you. Lack of confidence will."

The Colonel began marching back and forth, looking each of us in they eye, striking his swagger stick against his thigh.

"Don't be afraid of dying. God is not lazy He didn't make this wonderful world and then fail to make one just as great on the other side."

"The soldier is God's greatest creation. There is no greater honor than to die on the battlefield. To die during the heat of combat, is to die a true man in god's image: a warrior."

"Never be afraid of death on the battle field. There is no death for a warrior. You will live to fight again. As Saint Paul said, "the last enemy that shall be destroyed is death."

"Die a warrior, and you will be reborn a warrior. Die a coward, and you will be reborn a coward."

"And forget about luck. We make our own luck, good or bad. Our choices determine the future, how we live and die, not luck."

"Napoleon said, 'Fortune is a woman who must be wooed while she is in the mood.' I say, we make our own fortune, and if luck is a woman, she must be taken, overwhelmed, ravished, conquered; because if luck is a woman, she will not smile upon the man who lacks confidence, who doesn't have the guts to take action. Never put your faith in lady luck. Woman is fickle. So too is luck."

The Colonel stopped and stared me in the eye. "Do you think I'm funny? Do I amuse you?"

I kept eyes forward, said nothing, and wiped the smile from my face.

The Colonel, who was much taller than me, got right in my face: "Speak up you goddamned long haired sonofabitch."

I met his eyes: "I agree with the Colonel."

"You do? I'm so pleased. Flattered," he said. "Then enlighten us you pot smoking hippie bastard."

"Women respond to self-confidence. They are to be conquered. You don't beg a woman to submit," I replied.

"I'm not talking about women, you goddamned shit for brains dumb ass hippie!" he yelled. "Success in battle requires courage, discipline. Discipline, courage, not luck, will save your lives. Discipline will create a pattern of behavior that will allow you to respond immediately and reflexively to save your lives and kill the enemy."

The Colonel again began pacing, striking his swagger stick: "This unit, this training, our elite corps, will make higher demands on courage and discipline than any other branch of the service, at any other point in your lives."

The Colonel again faced us, standing ramrod straight. Lt Snake eyes stood behind him to the right.

"Success, to win each battle, depends on courage, discipline, initiative, and the brotherhood of loyalty, even more so than the weapons in your hands. Victory will be decided by those possessing the greatest courage and loyalty, not by dying for your country, but by making the other sonofabitch die for his country."

"Discipline requires obeying orders. If you men do not obey orders in small things, you cannot obey orders in big things and are incapable of fighting a successful battle."

The Colonel looked us up and down, again making eye contact with each of us. "Have I ever been afraid during battle? Of course. There is no dishonor in being afraid. In the heat of battle, there is terror. Anyone who says otherwise, is a liar."

"They say war is hell. Cowardice is a worse hell. A coward is always in hell, because he suffers a thousand deaths everyday. A brave man dies only once; but, he will live again."

"America is home of the brave, not the afraid! Like the enemy, fear must be conquered."

"There is no shame in feeling fear; but it takes courage to overcome your fears and your enemies. Your job is to make the enemy afraid, to instill a fear in him of the unknown, to terrorize his women, children, his very soul."

"You can't fight if you are afraid of getting killed. Wars are won only by killing. Only yellowbellies are afraid to die. There is no greater death, no greater honor than to die as a warrior on the battle field."

"Never retreat. Never give up. To retreat is as cowardly as it is fatal. Americans do not surrender."

"Never give up, never give in, never defend, always attack. Attack! Attack! Never think of defeat. Never think of retreat. Think only of killing the enemy."

You are going to grab the enemy by the nose, kick him in the ass, then blow his fucking brains out. Never take pity on your enemy. Never give him a chance to escape. Your job is to find him, kill him and leave no survivors."

"Remember, when you're tired, the enemy is just as tired. If you're afraid, he is more afraid. That's why, you must keep going. Never take counsel of your fears. Never fear death in combat. You have a greater chance of dying in your bed or being killed by a car."

"Therefore, in the heat of battle, we must always keep going forward, keep moving, forward, onward. Do not sit down to rest, do not think you can't do more. You can always do more. You can scream, throw a grenade, fire your weapon, raise hell; even if you think you're dying. Don't think about dying. Think about killing."

"You will fight as a unit. And yet, each of you must not just follow, but learn to lead, take charge, take the initiative. You must be an army of one."

"If you don't take the initiative, if you don't succeed, if you are not victorious, and don't die trying, there is no reason to come back alive. Failure is not an option. If you die on the battlefield, don't worry about your wives or girlfriends. Just think: how proud of you they'll be and what pretty widows they'll make."

"There is no point in surviving defeat. Our goal is to enter battle with complete confidence, purpose, resolution; only then shall we conquer, kill the enemy, and live long enough to achieve more glory."

The Colonel surveyed us all, turning his head slowly making eye contact with each of us, then he said, "We are in for a long war with a tough and determined enemy. We must be tough in mind, body and spirit. A pint of sweat will save a gallon of blood. Every man must run 2 miles with a full military pack. I'm talking about today. This exercise will be followed by a 12 mile hike. If you fail, if this is beyond your abilities, you will not survive tomorrow because its only going to get a lot tougher. We will start running at this point in 60 minutes. I will lead."

There were a few groans, some mutterings, but then everyone fell silent, intimidated by his steely glare.

"I have in my office," he said, his shoulders ramrod straight, "orders for the transfer of anyone who wants out now, and, I promise, you will be gone before the sun goes down."

The silence was total.

The Colonel turned smartly and marched to his office headquarters.

As for me --yours truly-- yes, I thought about leaving. Discipline? Spit and polish? Following orders? Surrounded by high adrenalin muscle bound skin-headed killers, who dream of dying a warriors' death and wiping out every Viet Cong in sight? I liked to fight; but only against bad guys. The Vietnamese never did me no harm. It was their country, not ours; and we didn't even want it. That war made no sense to me. No glory in it, that's for sure. I'd rather be on the beach with some babe. Unfortunately, leaving was not an option.

Lt Snake Eyes was now in charge, his narrow eyes upon us. He was tall, muscular, but had a thin pock-marked face, downturned mouth, and slits for eyes, which gave him the predatory look of a blonde-haired raptor with a buzz cut.

Later I learned Snake Eyes had been a Captain, about to be promoted to Major, then busted down to Lt, for allegedly committing a number of "illegal killings" in Vietnam. The two grunts who reported him, turned up missing, only to be found days later with their throats cut.

"At ease," Snake Eyes ordered.

Within seconds the other skin heads began mocking and calling me not so friendly names, such as: "Hey pussy!" "Cunt face!" "Long haired hippy freak," and asking, as they rubbed their crotch: "Are you a girl or a boy?" and "Come here homo and suck this!"

Snake Eyes said nothing, just gave me an icy stare. But not for long.

The Lt. called us to attention and said: "For the next 30 minutes, before gearing up for our walk in the park, to be led by the Colonel, you will receive basic instruction in attack and self-defense. I'm talking, hand to hand combat!"

Lt. Snake Eyes ordered "the hippie" --that's me-- to serve as a human punching bag in a karate demonstration.

Yeah, I had long hair, which The Company wanted me to keep. I'd taken drugs. But physically I was no "hippie." When I was eight year old my father had a swimming pool installed in our yard and I swam daily. At age 12, I devised my own set of barbells with a pipe connected to two cans of concrete and lifted weights seven days a week. Soon thereafter I began running two then four miles a day. In high school I was on the track team, and while still a freshman was promoted to the varsity football team where I played second then first string halfback. Although I found it boring, I also played baseball. I could pitch a mean fastball--an ability that must run in the family because my father and youngest brother could easily put one over the plate.

I wasn't a great athlete, certainly didn't have what it takes to compete at the college level--my brothers had that talent, not I. Even so, I was no 90 pound weakling.

I'd also been getting into fist fights since I was a kid. I liked fighting--but only in self-defense, or in defense of some under dog who was outnumbered--and no one beat me until one day my adversary threw a karate chop and hit me on the neck.

Thought he was going to slap me, and I laughed. Instead I lost all strength in the right half of my body and he kicked the crap out of me. I was 17. Weeks later, I began taking lessons in karate and kung fu.

So, I wasn't worried about keeping up with these guys. The proposed karate demonstration didn't make me shake with fear. Unfortunately, as Lt. Snake Eyes discussed personal combat techniques, and while giving verbal instructions, he suddenly hit me with a sucker-punch and tossed me down with a a leg-trip and arm-flip. Everyone laughed. Yeah, that was embarrassing.

The Lt. invited one of the skin-heads to practice the same technique on yours truly. But this time I was prepared, and with two deflecting blocks, a snap kick to the balls, and a chop to the neck, my adversary was down. Two more assholes suffered the same fate, and that's when the Lt. intervened to demonstrate the proper techniques. I was no match for him. He might have killed me if the Colonel, who apparently sees all and knows all, did not, over the camp loudspeaker, intervene. Nevertheless, point made: yours truly was no pussy. Even so, none of the skin heads wanted to be my friend and that was okay with me.

There followed a 2 mile run then a 12 mile hike with 50 pounds of gear strapped to our backs through very rough terrain, half of which was uphill--none of which was a problem for me. I left most of those suckers in the dust.

I decided to stick it out and not quit; as if I really had that option. Besides, two thousand a month plus expenses--courtesy of The Company-- was too good to pass up--certainly a lot better than being sent to Vietnam and coming home in a body bag. Turned out, I was misinformed about the Nam.

We trained in the mountains of North Carolina, then the swamps of Georgia, followed by two weeks of exercises in a desert camp midway between Los Angeles and western Arizona: 20,000 miles of arid desert, mountains, crags, cactus, mesquite and dry salt beds--all that remained of an ancient inland sea. Daytime temps over 130 degrees in the shade and freezing at night. They called it "Camp Patton," and "Little Libya." We were given minimal food and water, just one canteen a day.

"If you can survive and fight under these conditions," the Colonel promised, "you will have no difficulty killing any sonofabitch, no matter where he fights or hides."

The Big C had what he called the "King's throne" which could be in a helicopter, plane, or hilltop overlooking the training grounds which he would scrutinize with binoculars.

Every so often, he would get on the radio, or use a loud speaker to announce that so in so "is a damn good soldier" or that so and so "should stop acting like a woman or get the hell out of here!"

Sometimes we'd go 36, 48 hours without sleep. Men fell from exhaustion, heat-stroke, and rattlesnakes. At least a dozen quit.

It was arduous, physically and mentally, no doubt about it. Field training, map reading, individual land navigation after parachuting into the unknown, 12-man team exercises carrying telephone poles or cars and jeeps through sand, mud, water, or up mountain roads; training in strategy, tactics, planning, reconnaissance deployment, camouflage, infiltration, survival, escape, resistance, evasion, kidnapping, interrogation, guerrilla and unconventional warfare, sabotage, counterinsurgency, urban operations, martial arts, advanced marksmanship and live fire maneuvers; endless drilling, saluting, field exercises, spit and polish; and lots of classroom instruction followed by field training to make sure what we'd learned would be memorized and put to use.

Although I had never taken a fancy to hunting, I liked guns and was good with a pistol, revolver, and rifle--almost always hitting exactly where I aimed.

On the second day of training at the camp in North Carolina, and while lying in the mud, engaged in target practice with rifle and scope, I calmly put one bullet after another dead center in a human-shaped target, going through the same hole in the middle of the bulls' eye. I'd had a lot of practice: not only with guns, but rocks and baseballs. I hit what I aimed at. Accurately firing a stabilized rifle with scope at a target 100 yards away was child's play. And, it helped that I was farsighted.

Six shots, all bulls eyes, through the same little hole.

As I slipped the next round in the chamber, the Colonel, a pair of binoculars hanging from his neck, marched over and yelled: "What the hell are you doing?"

Lt Snake Eyes was right behind him.

"Sir! Trying to hit the center," I answered.

"Like hell you are," the Colonel barked. "You're trying to kill some sonofabitch before he can kill you. Aim at the target. At the body! Forget the head. Aim at the center, goddamn it. Hitting him in the body will always do the trick. So get that long goddam sissy hair out of your goddamn eyes and hit the target. If you can't do that, maybe we'll get you a broom and a mop, something more suitable for your talents."

"Sir! I am shooting dead center."

The Colonel squinted his eyes and stared at the distant target "You goddamn pot smoking hippie! You never even came close. There's no holes in that target."

"He's not fit to be in this unit, sir!" Lt. Snake Eyes added dryly.

"Give me that rifle, you near sighted bastard," the Colonel demanded.

"Wait a minute," I replied.

"No one gave you permission to speak," the Lt. barked.

"I've hit that fucking target dead center every fucking time," I insisted.

"That's it, you're out of here," the Lt said sternly. "You're finished. I'm writing you up for violation of Article 89. Insubordination talking back to an officer."

"This is bull shit," I said, standing up. "I'm a better shot than you two assholes combined."

The Lt took a step toward me. I took a fighting stance.

"Wait a minute, you goddam hippie sonofabitch!" The Colonel ordered.

The Colonel put the binoculars to his eyes. "What the hell? Let's check that target."

I didn't need the binoculars. I hit dead center in the little black dot six times. Bull Eye. Easy as pie with a scope and stabilized rife.

The Colonel and the Lt., followed by yours truly, marched over to the target. "Well, I'll be goddamned," the Colonel said in surprise.

Sure enough, one little slit, dead center. The Colonel dug in the backdrop with a knife, and: Bulls eye, dead center, six times, all through the same slit at 100 yards.

The Colonel apologized. Later the Colonel called me into his office and suggested I should enroll in sniper school. Nah--wasn't interested. As to Article 89? All forgotten. Apparently the Colonel had respect for those with the courage to stand up to him when he was wrong--even if they were a "long haired hippie sonofabitch."

The Lt. was not a man with forgiveness in his heart. He did not like me. No doubt about it. He made a special point of ridiculing and targeting me for extra details and all manner of abuse. Hey. I took it. Not going to argue with a barking dog when he's got power of life and death over yours truly.

After six weeks of that hell, next stop: Vietnam. Our mission? A shaman living in a remote jungle village. The result? Clusterfuck.

One week later, I'm back in California, on my way to Palo Alto, and Project ULTRA.

I never thought I'd see "Lt. Snake Eyes" again.

That was then. This was now. It was a bad sign that Snake Eyes was on my Sonora trail and had probably been following me for the last 3 weeks. Why him? Goddam it! And how were they tracking me? I gazed skyward and wondered about satellites: could they see me, my car, from space?

As to why; well that was obvious: they hoped I'd lead them to a sorcerer.

"Evil follows you," Sophia had said.

I retrieved my Colt 45 and holstered it between the front seats.

"Follow the heart," Sophia had advised.

I studied the map. The heart of the Sonora River Valley encompassed hundreds of square miles extending from Banámichi to Arizpe to Chinapa to Bacoachi and beyond, all along highway 89. don Rojas's ranchero had to be somewhere in the vicinity of Banámichi and Bacoachi! Still this was a lot of ground to cover.

Each little town, however, could provide clues. I was certain that some of the natives had to know of don Rojas or his lovely daughter, especially the young bucks. Maybe one of them could give me directions.

Putting the VW in gear I pulled out into highway 15... turned East on highway 14... and an hour later turned left on highway 89. I continued north-east toward Banámichi, Arizpe, Chinapa and Bacoachi, the latter of which was maybe 5 hours distant from the Cantina, the same amount of time as when don Rojas and I were "speed reading" to his hacienda.

I arrived at Banámichi before evening. It was a very small town, there were a few handsome, muscular vaqueros on horseback, and here and there, a lovely Señorita, some alone, others walking in twos, arm-in-arm, their heads covered with shawls. I found a bar and restaurant which also served as a hotel, outside of which were parked a few pickups, motorcycles, and two horses hitched to a rail. There were two men at the bar, another alone at a table alone, and three men-- tough, hard, mean-looking hombres-- sitting together wearing cowboy hats and checkered shirts, eating and drinking coffee and who looked up looked up and stared when I walked in.

I gave the three vaqueros a glance, tipped my cowboy hat in greeting, and took a seat at a small table. They proceeded to ignore me.

The owner-bar-tender, a man with a big belly, fat cheeks, and handle-bar mustache, was all smiles until he heard the name "don Rojas." I thought he was going to spit on the floor, in disgust. Instead, he handed me a menu, turned his back and exited through the swinging doors which led to the kitchen.

It was a nice place, clean, lots of flowers, paintings of pastoral scenes from old Mexico on the wall, and of course, Coca Cola signs and a framed picture of Jesus. On the other side of an arched open doorway which led to a beautifully bricked garden courtyard and shaded patio, I spied a plump, but very pretty teenaged girl sweeping the floor. She gave me a glance, walked to the kitchen, and a few moments later emerged carrying a tray of nachos, peanuts, water, and two small paper cups, one with green guacamole the other red hot sauce, which she set on my table. I gave her my most charming smile. If the girl laid off the enchiladas and tacos and lost 30 pounds, she would have been a total Foxy Lady!

The youngest of the three tough-looking vaqueros, a tall skinny fellow, with an angry knife cut across his face, gave her a toothy grin, and called out: "Maria!" She ignored him but smiled with pleasure.

Five minutes later she returned with my order: slow roasted pork, cream tomatillo, chipatte holandaise, and roasted pasilla chile. The food was delicious! Lucky for me, I only put a speck of the red hot sauce to my tongue: thought my mouth had been set on fire!

When Maria returned, I asked if she knew "Sophia Rojas."

For a brief moment, Maria's face lit up with pleasure: "Sofia? Sí, ella es muy hermosa!"

"When did you see her last? ¿Cuando fue la ultima vez que la viste?" I asked. "Does she come here often?

A look of sorrow crossed Maria's face. "No. No más. Porque mi hermano."

"She stopped coming because of your brother?" I asked. "Why?"

"Si." Maria replied. "Sophia only come dos veces. Two times. Mi hermano, Miguel, he like her too much, I think."

"He dated here twice, then what happened?" I asked.

"Mi hermano, él la ve. ¡Enamorarse! Pero eso fue hace muchos años," Maria informed me.

"Your brother, Miguel, fell in love with her?" I asked.

"Si. Mucho amor. ¡Amor loco! He got love sick." she answered sadly. "He was very handsome. Strong. But the love sickness make him weak, sick, not strong."

"Where is Miguel? ¿Dónde está tu hermano? I'd like to talk with him."

"Se muda a Los Angeles. Él tiene un trabajo en América," she answered. "Él está. He mucho mejor, better now."

"Miguel is in Los Angeles, eh? Well, then, do you know where Sophia lives?" I asked.

"No. Mi padre dice que es una bruja. Mi padre, he say Sophia, peligrosa, dangerous. A bruja."

"Sophia is a dangerous witch, eh? Is there anyone in this town how might know where she lives?" I asked.

The waitress shook her head, no.

The scar-faced Mexican vaquero, still wearing his cowboy hat got up, sauntered over to me and said: "Si. Sophia. I know her! Si!"

Smiling, he used his hands to fashion the shape of a well endowed beauty and then said: "Sophia Rojas! Ella es una perra arrogante. ¿Por qué la buscas? A ella no le gustan los gringos yanquis."

Sophia is an arrogant stuck-up bitch who hates Yankees, so I best forget about her, is what he was saying.

"I have a message for her father, don Rojas. I have no interest in Sophia. Do you know where she lives? don Roja's ranchero? Hacienda?" I asked. "¿Sabes dónde vive? Su ranchero? "

The cowboy asked me for a "cigarrillo," but I had none. Instead I pulled out a 20 dollar bill. He took it.

"Si" he answered. "Hay un camino, a road, va a Los Hoyas. Sophia, Aquí es donde ella vive, creo."

"Take the road to Los Hoyas? I asked?

"Si."

Back at my car, checking my map I couldn't see any road linking highway 89 with Los Hoyas which was way over on highway 17; nowhere near the "heart."

Back inside, I showed the map to the scar-faced vaquero. He removed his hat and scratched his head. I handed him another $20.00, and he pointed at a spot about 5 miles north of Banámichi. Then he pointed at another spot.

"Same road," he said. "To Sophia, Los Hoyas."

Back outside, I studied the map. The turn off he'd indicated was a few miles north, looped east, then north, then looped south through the river valley and ended up going west, forming a half-circle and reconnecting with highway 89 about 50 miles north of Banámichi, just below Sinoquipe.

I had maybe two hours of day light left. Even if the scar-faced vaquero was full of shit, I could check out that side road, find a place to camp, and sample the magical ingredients inside the remaining three satchels.

I made sure I wasn't being followed and found the turn off. There was no indication it led to Los Hoyas, but I took it anyway, then waited 20 minutes. No evidence I was being followed. The turn off was lined with pine and oak, and weaved up and down around hills both big and small, toward then away from various river tributaries. It was in bad condition, lots of potholes, sections with no pavement but only hard packed dirt. It was rather isolated. No traffic, just turn offs leading who knows where, probably to some isolated ranch. Increasingly, I was getting a bad feeling.

Just as I was going round a bend surrounded by a small forest of scrub oak and deciduous trees a dark skinned Mexican with a Fu-Manchu mustache and dressed in cowboy boots and hat, stepped into the roadway, sporting a rifle pointed right at me. There were blood stains on his shirt and white cotton pants.

I came to a halt. One glance took in the entire scene: Up ahead, to my right, a station wagon, Arizona license plates, parked off road in a small clearing, the trunk and all four doors open, a dark-haired Mexican searching inside; a fat man wearing a dirty cowboy hat rummaging through open suitcases and belongings which had been dumped on the ground; a White man, blonde hair, bloodied, no shirt, tied up and laid up next to a tree, body burnt, stabbed, maybe shot, head lolling to the side; a White boy, face down, also dead, his pants and shorts pulled down, his butt blood smeared; two Mexicans, a fat one raping a blonde White woman, the other, a skinny dude doing a blonde teenage girl as a third fat pig of a man wearing a sombrero and drinking from a bottle of tequila, playfully kicked the skinny rapist in the ass shouting "Ándale! Ándale! A la mierda con esa puta y listo. Mi turno. No tomes todo el día.."

There were two beat up pickup trucks about 30 yards distant from each other and parked off road also to my right. The pickups had most likely been used to box in that family, tourists no doubt, who'd foolishly taken this turnoff. Or, maybe, like me, they'd been given bull shit directions at the last town!

No chance for me to back up and get the hell out of there. The Mexican in front was using my head as a bulls eye. A glance in the rearview mirror confirmed that a very skinny Mexican, wearing a baseball cap, armless blood-smeared t-shirt, his face and arms marked with tattoos, had stepped out of the woods about 25 yards behind me. Mr Tattoo had a rifle pointed at the back of my head. Adding to my troubles, another Mexican, a big fat hombre, holding a pistol and a bottle of tequila had exited one of the two beat up pickup trucks to join Mr. Fu-Manchu who blocked my way.

These were some very bad hombres. Killers, cutthroats, rapists and thieves; and to guess what they had in store for yours truly, didn't take a PhD.

Mr. Fu-Manchu, to the front of me, joined now by the pistol-packing Mr. Tequila, motioned with his rife barrel, indicating I should park my car off road. I wasn't going to do that. Lucky for me, I had holstered my Colt 45 in the space between the front seats.

Putting up both hands, I nodded my head toward the driver's side door, then slowly dropped my left hand toward the door handle while staring forward. I glanced in the rearview mirror. Mr. Tattoo had lazily lowered his rifle. Big mistake.

Slowly swinging open the door I dropped my right and pulled out my 45, and in one motion slowly stepped out of the car and through the open window shot both those fuckers right in the chest. Swinging round, I fired my 45 at Mr. Tattoo; missed his abdomen but blowing off his left lower leg. Down he fell.

Next: the fat SOB who'd been waiting his turn to rape the blonde teenager. Fat fool had a tequila bottle in one hand, a revolver in the other which he fired missing me entirely. I fired: bang, a small hole in the front of his head, his brains splattering out the back.

The two dudes ransacking the station wagon and suitcases took off on the run, one jumping out a side door opposite, making it impossible to get a clear shot, and the second hombre running around the station wagon, and, goddamn it, I fired and missed him.

The two who'd been raping the women were desperately pulling up their pants and fumbling for their guns. I calmly walked forward and killed them both, striking one in the chest, the other in the face, a cloud of blood drifting in the air as he toppled to the ground.

I noticed, then, what appeared to be a bloodied doll, split in two, an arm and a leg torn off and cast in the dirt.

Fucking A. It was a baby--they must have grabbed its arms and legs and ripped it in half. Sick fucks!

don Rojas was wrong about one thing: No need to journey to other dimensions to find devils and demons. This planet already had plenty.

The naked, blonde teenaged girl had curled up into a ball and was crying, then screaming. Her mother was whimpering, but lay face down, clutching the dirt.

Ignoring their cries, I carefully walked in the direction taken by the two hombres who'd run away. The sound of breaking branches and twigs confirmed they were not waiting in ambush but were heading for the river to make their escape.

Problem was, I couldn't let those two hombres get away or they'd come back with all their friends, relatives, the police, and hunt me down before I got out of Mexico; and that would be the end of yours truly.

My 45 held 8 bullets, and had one slug remaining. There were two fully loaded cartridges in the trunk. These were quickly retrieved. But first the brain case of Mr. Tattoo required a going away present. True, he was in shock, and would probably bleed out, but, why take chances? Bang!

Turned out Mr. Tattoo was carrying a beautiful Bowie-Axe throwing knife. On a whim, I took that with me. Then I ran like hell into the woods, reloading and intending to flank and intercept those two fleeing desperados and kill them both.

Running at an angle to the direction they'd run, ducking branches, leaping over big rocks and fallen trees, I made it to the river--probably 200 yards away from the rapes and murders. Cutting to my right, along the river bank, moving slowly, quietly, listening intently, then: voices, water splashing.

One of the killers, a fat bastard, was sitting on his big ass, next to a tree, removing his shoes, a pistol cradled in his lap. The other, a skinny dude, was already 20 yards out, almost waist deep in the river, struggling sideways then forward then sideways against the current, his shoes in one hand, a gun in the other. It might take two shots to get him as he kept slipping and moving erratically. If I missed, or shot the fat fucker first, Mr. Skinny might dive down, and then I'd be up shit creek. If I'm shooting at the skinny, the fat bastard next to the tree might get me with a lucky shot.

I let fly with the Bowie-Axe, and, goddam it, the knife struck the tree an inch above the fat man's head. He leaned his head back and looked up at the knife, his eyes wide with surprise. No time to think about it. Shot him in the chest, then wheeled around to get Mr. Skinny who, thank god, made no attempt to dive beneath the water but only struggled that much faster through the rushing river in a desperate attempt to get away.

One blast, then a second, and he was face down with splash. Did I miss? Twice? Wading out into the river I nearly intercepted him as he floated by, face up--or, rather, no face up, as he had no face at all--the bullet entering the back of his head and blowing out his brains and face, leaving only an empty bloody cavern.

The Colt 45 is a powerful gun. I love it!

Retrieving the knife and shell casings, I ran like hell, back toward my car, thinking, planning what to do next.

Now I had another problem: those two women.

When I was shooting those fucks, the blonde teenager looked right at me as she screamed and cried. She'd be able to identify me, my car, and give a complete description of yours truly.

I'd been well trained: No witnesses. Kill them all.

I rather enjoyed killing those eight bandidos. A super adrenalin rush! But innocent women?

Fuckin' A! Didn't like that idea at all.

Maybe killing the women would be merciful, but, no, not going to do that. Has to be another way.

Rapidly approaching the killing fields, still 40 yards distant, I came to a sudden halt, alerted by a car's engine: A vehicle had pulled up and turned off the motor.

Fuck me! How many more of these guys do I have to kill?

Closer I crept, gun in hand.

Fuck me!

A black jeep was parked next to my VW. Snake Eyes and another skin-head dude I recognized from the Institute, had spread out, guns drawn. They were carefully checking out the scene, and examining the bodies. Both were wearing black leather gloves.

Snake Eyes approached the weeping teenaged girl who was sitting in the dirt, her arms clasped across her chest, rocking back and forth and crying pitifully. She looked up at him with hope in her eyes.

He came closer, put his fingers to his lips: "shhhh," he said calmly, then taking hold of her head, gave it a snap, and she toppled over dead.

The mother, still naked, was crawling, painfully, to who knows where. Snake Eyes walked up, too hold of her head, and also gave her the coupe de grasse.

I watched as Snake Eyes and the other skin head dragged and arranged the bodies of the dead Mexicans, pour tequila on them, and retrieve two of the guns and a rifle which lay in the dirt. At point blank range and using these weapons, they shot several more holes into each of the dead men and dropped the guns and rifles next to the bodies.

Snake Eyes and his skin-head partner then leaned against the hood of my VW, waiting.

I remembered the other skin head from the Institute. He stayed in the same dorm as me. He was crazy. Violently crazy. I thought he was a schizophrenic. He was a veteran, had been wounded several times, and in his last battle died on the battle field and came back to life. He was one of the psychic warriors who'd gone nuts. Why the hell was he here?

There were a number of nut jobs back at the Institute sleeping in the dorm, all undergoing psychic warriors' training. Two pimply-faced teenagers, and several old women--two of whom looked like worn-out street whores and the other like a kindly grandmother--were among the "trainees," each of them supposedly a "witch."

A very tall thin ugly looking dude with long black greasy hair and also staying at the dorm, introduced himself as a "warlock." He hung out with two older men, also trainees, claiming to be wizards.

Another schizophrenic, a swishy flaming faggot, said he was the reincarnation of Cassandra, the daughter of King Priam of ancient Troy. "I can see the future!" he claimed. "The skies are on fire and the great cities shall be swallowed by the rising seas."

Then there were the so-called "psychics" who claimed to have ESP, could read minds, and predict one's future; including a petite and very pretty long-haired blonde teenager. She was a sexy thing!

Truth is, at first I was attracted to the blonde teen who may have been as old as 21; liked her fox face and sexy body. Wanted to do her, and would have happily taken her to bed, if she hadn't turned out to be a nasty bitch. Of course, some women are bitchy because they are checking the man's courage. Only losers run away.

When we finally had a chance to talk, she put on her bitch-face, and told me "I'm psychic. I can read minds. Can you read minds? I bet you can't. You don't look special at all. Only special people, with the gift, can read minds," she'd said.

"I'm more interested in what a woman doesn't mind," I answered.

Then she said: "Give me a dollar?"

"For what?" I asked.

"The vending machines. I'm hungry. Give me a dollar," she answered, her hand out, palm up.

"And what do I get in return?" I asked, giving her my most dashing smile.

"Nothing. Haven't you heard of chivalry? I need a dollar," she answered.

"Well, if you are really psychic, and can read minds," I answered, "then you should have known I wasn't going to give you any money."

Giving me the middle finger, she stormed off.

These "trainees" were all paid volunteers, I learned. On the fast track to becoming "psychic warriors." And like me, were staying in the dorm.

I wondered how many of the "psychic warriors" from the Institute might have also traveled to Mexico, along with Lt. Snake Eyes. And if so, why?

Lt. Snake eyes, and his skin-head partner continued to lean against my car, waiting. Finally, I emerged from the woods with my 45 in hand, even though they'd holstered their weapons.

I stopped. Met the eyes of both. Waited.

They looked at each other, got into their jeep, and drove away.

I walked around admiring their handy work in the dimming sunlight. It looked like these dead assholes killed each other. Even my shell casings were gone.

Too bad about the women. But, after the nightmare they'd gone through, the hellish memories they'd have to live with; maybe it was a merciful death. I stabbed their dead bodies with the throwing knife and wiping away my prints, dropped it on the ground.

After backing up my VW and turning around, I got out and used a tree branch to erase any tracks, then drove away in the direction opposite to Snake Eyes; thinking, planning, and worrying about having those two skin heads on my trail.

How did I feel about killing those eight bandidos? Good! Pleased! Proud! Satisfied! Excited! It was a super adrenalin rush! A feeling of great accomplishment.

Demons and devils deserve to die. There are a lot of men who need killin'.

Years later, I was asked, once: "How many men have you killed?" When it comes to devils like these? Not enough!

6. Owl Woman and the Warlock

I continued driving, looping over hills and up and down darkening valleys, toward and then away from the river. Finally, I found a dirt road turn off twenty miles from the scene of the crime. There was no indication it led to Los Hoyas, but as the sun was sinking low I took it anyway

I found a clearing near the river, semi-surrounded and protected by a grove of scrub oak and deciduous trees. Five minutes later, had the camp site up, food water gun by my side, fire starting to flame, three satchels beckoning. Gazing into the sky, at the full moon up above, I thought: All I need is love! Or, maybe not!

Gazing at the satchel, I was seriously considering discovering what may lay behind magic doors five, six and seven. But the vibes weren't right. After the excitement and adrenalin high of just an hour ago, I now felt jittery, nervous, a little depressed. I also didn't want to be trippin' into some alternate reality, only to have the Lt and that other skin head come knockin' on the door. Not understanding how they were able to follow and find me, was discomforting for sure.

Did I really want to lead those two skin heads to don Rojas and Sophia?

To work off my jittery nerves, and before it became completely dark, I decided, gun in hand, to probe and search the surroundings, do some basic reconnaissance, and set up a perimeter with string tied low and attached to leafy branches and encompassing my car and the surrounding circle of trees Thirty minutes later, I felt safe, secure, isolated and alone, with only croaking frogs, chirping insects, and singings birds to keep me company; confident no skin heads, bandidos, demons, warlocks, or witches were hiding in the bushes, and there was nothing that might eat me while I slept.

Settling down near the fire, with log book in hand, I began detailing the days' events while simultaneously pondering, in the back of my mind, the decisions to be made and possibilities that lay before me. At the top of my agenda: Finding Sophia and don Rojas.

Two hours later, notes complete, I gazed again at the three satchels which seemed to beckon: Eat me. Smoke me!

What the hell! Why not? But first, and despite the darkening forest, I decided to again reconnoiter the surroundings.

Twenty minutes later, gazing upon the contents of the three satchels, I couldn't decide which to smoke, drink, or eat. Finally, a choice was made: none of the above.

Instead, rereading my notes, and recalling the teaching of don Rojas, I took a meditative lotus posture, eyes closed, mind focused and created an image of his hacienda, then the book-lined shelves, the dinning table, don Rojas at the head, Sophia sitting across from me. Focus. Focus. Remote viewing, here I come. Picturing in my mind's eye: I recalled the hacienda from every angle when we first drove up, the tour of the surroundings, and sought to visualize what it might appear like from above, higher, higher still, as if miles above it all, looking down and visualizing the geography, the river, nearby roads...

... and then I began thinking of Sophia, remembering our night together, making love...how I'd love to hold her in my arms... kiss her lips... and... and there went my concentration and futile attempts at "remote viewing." The location of the hacienda, remained a mystery.

Exhausted, I stretched out on the sleeping bag, fell into a deep sleep, and began to dream.

Dreams being dreams, those which flittered through my sleeping mind's eye were many-splendored, prismatic, variegated, a motley of multi-colored scenes jumbled together in an incoherent narrative of visual images... an upside down crucifix becoming the arms and legs of a baby in the hands of laughing fat men as they tore the screaming infant in half, tossing scraps to s naked blonde teenage girl getting fucked by a hooded priest whose face becomes a grinning skull in the hand of the Shaman emerging from his jungle hut, becoming a shadow with knife lunging, I fire my gun the dead man falls then rises up becomes the Shaman becomes a hooded priest lying in a baby's basinet, which dream-like became a faceless corpse drifting in the flowing river only to sit up holding an upside down crucifix which explodes in flame, from which emerged a burning dragon flying into a steaming jungle and gazing down at a six man team led by the Lt. snaking through a wet tunnel of surrounding vegetation and trees, a Vietnamese village, gun shots, a man down, the Shaman becoming don Rojas, emerging from his hut swinging a grinning skull becoming flesh and flaming eyes of a hood priest... becoming a faceless corpse floating down a river, in which a naked Sophia is swimming, then standing, then becoming the alternate reality demon princess queen gazing into a mirror reflecting Sophia's face... they embrace, kiss, faced me laughing, twins of day and night, good and evil, merging into one her face becoming death, rotting flesh, skeletal bone...a skull becomes the hooded priest becomes don Rojas becomes Sophia naked, lusting, stepping forward, kissing me passionately, wrapping her long legs around me... we are making love...her hands clawing into my chest...

I sat up. A black crow was standing on my chest. It cocked its head to the left and right staring at me as I stared back. And then, with a girlish-human-like cackle, the crow laughed, flapped its wings, and was gone.

Oh fuck me! Deja vu all over again.

Opening my eyes, sitting up, expecting the now familiar Pemex gas station, I saw instead, trees, my camp site, and the dawn sun rising.

Had the black-crow-Sophia really landed on my chest, or had it just been part of the dream? No idea.

A 30 minute run along the road side, followed by a swim in the river: my morning ablutions complete, I began searching the VW for anything out-of-the-ordinary that could serve as a transmitter or tracking device. Eureka! Found it under the left rear wheel well spliced to a wire connecting the battery to the break lights. How it worked, I had no idea, other than what Peter had told me back at the Institute: the same technology that enabled physicists to track and locate the Soviet Union's 1958, sputnik satellite as it orbited Earth, could be used in reverse, to track and locate someone's position on Earth. All it took was a properly equipped satellite with reception and transmission capabilities.

Tossing the device into the forest, I packed up camp, turned the car around, headed west, then south, and an hour later emerged on highway 89 a few miles north of Banámichi. From there, it was onward north-east toward Arizpe, Chinapa and Bacoachi,

What about Los Hoyas? No. I think not. That razor-slashed vaquero must have been feeding me rooster and bovine feces.

The first town I stopped at was interesting. There were handsome looking vaqueros on horseback and some slim, and very lovely Senoritas, one of whom gave me an enticing smile only to be shepherded away by a disapproving matron, probably her mother. The little town's main attraction was the plaza with it's clock tower and the splendid architecture of the Nuestra Senora de la Asunción Temple. Another little Church lay south of the town. There were only two restaurants, and at one, I struck gold.

The proprietress, a beautiful Señora with flashing black eyes and a diamond on her finger, was tempting, buxom, sexy, flirtatious, and knew how to swing her hips and bend low to give a glimpse of her cleavage when serving my breakfast. I thought about paying her a visit maybe after sundown--but those hopes were dashed when this big dude, looked like an Apache Indian, cowboy hat set rakishly to the side, sleeves rolled up displaying muscular arms, stepped into the dinning room; the big smile on his chiseled face disappearing as he gave me, then her, then me a "look" with menacing hatchet-throwing eyes.

He took a seat, watching.

The proprietress, her conduct now quite reserved, said she knew of don Rojas--a healer who could bring rain. But where he lived, she did not know, directing me instead to the local padre; and then, on second thought, "la enfermera at Cruz Roja." A nurse

Quickly finishing my breakfast I headed for the little Church and as I got closer, had this bad feeling. I stopped, checked my surroundings: no bandidos only two ugly, ghastly old women dressed in black, who, as they passed by, stared boldly in my eyes then looked me up and down, as if sizing me up for dinner. They were coming from the Church, but the vibrations they gave off were pure evil.

Stepping inside, I noted the burning candles, rows of wooden pews, a confessional, the plaster statues of the Virgin Mary and baby Jesus, and the tortured Jesus hanging from a cross behind the wooden altar---but, no priest or parishioners. Heard a door open, and a little peasant boy, barefoot, dressed in white cotton shirt and pants, emerged from the rectory, his cherubic face wet with tears.

"Dónde puedo encontrar al padre?" I asked. "Do you know where I can find the padre?"

The little boy, glanced up, his mouth and lips swollen and red; then looked at the floor as he pointed in the direction from which he came.

I stepped into the rectory. Pictures of Jesus and the crucification on the wall, writing desk, rumpled cot, wash basin, wet towel, priestly robes on a hanger, but no priest!

One door leads to the next and the second door was in back and slightly ajar. Pushing it open I walked into a darkened room reeking of cigarettes, sweat, and unwashed decay, and illuminated only by feeble candlelight. The padre, his right hand engaged in an up and down motion, had his back to me and was facing the wall where hung an upside down Jesus on a crucifix. On a little wooden table sat a skull with a flaming candle set upon the crown, a knife and pieces of frog and snake, and a little jar with who knows what inside. Old books and a human jaw bone lay upon another little table set against the wall. On the wall to my left were old newspaper clippings with headlines announcing murders, terrible accidents, and death, and on my right there were old posters with photos of missing children and offerings of rewards. And stacked in piles and laying on the floor, porno magazines, hard-core shit featuring sadism and torture, and sonofabitch: kiddie porn!

This sick fuck couldn't be the priest.

"Perdóneme," I said. "I'm looking for the padre. Eres el padre?"

He jumped, yelling "Meirda!" in surprise, then spun around, his disheveled black hair greasy, face radiating evil, curled lips in a snarl, eyes flaming red.

"Quién diablos eres? Qué coño quieres?" he demanded angrily as he zipped up his pants.

"Do you speak English?" I asked. "Are you the padre?"

The priest's eyes turned a pale ice blue: "Si. Who are you?"

"Nice place you have here," I said with a sweep of my hand. "I'm trying to locate a medicine man. His name is don Rojas."

The priest's eyes widened in surprise. "don Rojas hombre muy malo! Very bad man. He cause great evil. All this," the priest said with a wave of his hand, "is the evil work of el demonio don Rojas, may his soul burn in hell."

I eye-balled the decor, magazines, newspaper clippings--could this really be the handiwork of don Rojas? No. No. I was sure the priest was jerking off to the upside down Jesus. Now I was starting to wonder about that little boy with the tears in his eyes. No--I rejected that thought out-of-hand. No way a priest would do that to a little kid.

Taking out my wallet, I said to the priest: "I'm willing to pay if you can tell me where don Rojas lives and how to get there."

"How much you pay? Why you want this evil diablo?" the priest asked stepping close. His breath was rank, putrid.

"I have a message for him, that's all." I opened my wallet and pulled out two twenties and a ten. "I can give you fifty dollars."

The priest looked at the money then me, like I was trying to hand him dog shit.

He said: "I can give you one thousand American dollars if you help me to kill this diablo, don Rojas, and send him to hell."

"Sorry. I'm not a killer," I replied.

The priest gave me an evil smile then snarled. "Si. You are a killer!"

"Sorry, no can do," I answered. "That's not my bag!"

"Then fuck you and get out, before I send you to hell!" he yelled, picking up a knife which he waved at me menacingly.

Friendly dude!

I left the nice priest and went in search of the nurse.

Cruz Roja was not much of a hospital, but a four room adobe which was little more than a waiting area, examining room and surgery. The little hospital was adorned with pictures of Jesus, posters of the human body and internal organs, a Coca Cola wall clock, and crowded with white chipped cabinets, medical tools and implements, wooden chairs, and a small bed for patients to lie on.

The enfermera was busily setting and bandaging the broken leg of a handsome vaquero who'd been kicked by a mule. Plump, friendly, but all business, the enfermera served as the facility's only nurse and doctor, though, I quickly learned she had a degree in neither. The "hospital" did not earn much money as most patients had little or none, she told me, and was funded by the Red Cross and a mystery benefactor.

"Si," she knew don Rojas. She and others in the surrounding towns and villages had sought his healing magic over the years.

"You believe in magic?" I asked.

"Si. The power of belief, creencia, the power of suggestion, el poder de la sugerencia puede sanar. Mucho mejor. Feel much better. Si. don Rojas has powerful medicine! Si!"

"Do you think don Rojas is an evil man?" I asked.

"No," she answered. "He is good man. Kind. Generous."

Unfortunately, the enfermera didn't know where don Rojas resided.

"Then how do you contact him?" I asked.

The enfermera made the sign of the cross. "Una bruja. La mujer búho."

"The owl woman? She's a witch?" I asked.

"Si."

"And how do I find her?" I asked.

"Debes hablar con su nieta. Her granddaughter."

"I must speak with her granddaughter. What's her name? Where can I find her?"

The enfermera wrote out the grandmother's name, then the girl's name and street and city where she lived. I'd already been there twice: Bañamichi!

Twenty minutes later, after gassing up and getting additional directions at the local Pemex station, I parked in the dirt driveway of a small ranchero and was soon knocking on the door. I waited while chickens and pigs wondered the front yard and two curious dogs sniffed my legs then sat and watched. There were crops growing in the fields, a stable with two big horses, fruit-laden trees, and a colorful garden out front.

A pretty little girl opened the door a crack and gazed at me curiously.

"Is Senorita Itotia Citali at home? I asked.

A moment later a dark haired teenaged beauty came to the door dressed in sandals, blue jeans cut off at thigh level and wearing an embroidered white peasant blouse which gave a tantalizing hint as to the size and shape of her splendid breasts.

"Sí. ¿Puedo ayudarlo?" she asked.

"Yes, I'd like to speak to Senorita Itotia Citali."

"I'm Dancing Star!" she answered. "What do you want?"

"You speak English?" I asked.

"Of course. I was born in Arizona. I go to the university there," she answered.

"I'm trying to locate a man by the name of don Rojas. I've been told that your grandmother is the only one who knows where he lives."

"My grandmother? Which one?"

"Ichhtaca Ihuicatl," I answered.

"She's not my grandmother."

"No?" I asked.

"She's my great great grandmother. Ichhtaca Ihuicatl Tonalnan, which means Secret Sky Mother of Light." Dancing Star looked surreptitiously over her shoulder and stepped outside: "She's a witch, you know! A bruja!"

"Great Great grandmother? Is she still alive?" I asked. "Does she live here?"

"Not here. Would you like me to take you? she asked.

"Sure. Wonderful! Where's she live?" I asked.

"Near Chinapa. Let's go in your car. Wait! Let me get my things," she said.

"Wow! Okay," I answered.

I watched her delightful little butt disappear back in the house. And, of course, I thought about doing her. What a tasty little babe!

Five minutes later, she was out the door with a bulging shopping bag in one hand, her purse in the other, and we were on our way.

"What's in the bag," I asked, wondering if it contained assorted magic.

"Cleaning supplies," she said. "I'm here on summer break," she said. "And I've been so bored! I can't wait to get back to Phoenix. There's absolutely nothing to do here. But my father, he's so old fashioned, and my mother misses me so much, and my girlfriend, Tricia, she said I should be more independent but I don't know, I think she just needs me and that's why she wants me to stay in Phoenix. She has a boyfriend and she's so in love but I think he's wrong for her and he makes her cry and that's why..."

I gave her a sidelong glance. What a chatter box!

Kicking off her sandals she put her cute little bare feet up on the dashboard. Nice legs! I wanted to touch them, run my hands up her thighs and beneath those tight cutoff jeans and... but kept my hands and thoughts to myself.

"Tell me about your great great grandmother," I said. "How do you know she's a witch?"

"Oh she's a witch, alright. They call her Owl Woman, because when she was young like me, she could change into an owl and fly at night.

"Is she a good witch?" I asked.

"Oh yes! She practiced good magic to cure people, and could conjure spirits, and protect against evil spells, or free people from bewitchment by evil witches."

"How does she do that?"

"Songs, prayers, chants, spells, potions. When she was young she would go out at night as a spirit, sometimes with her daughter and granddaughter--they were witches too-- and they'd join other good witches to curse, cast spells, call demons, and do battle against evil witches," she explained.

"Are you a witch?" I asked.

"I wish!" she answered.

"Why not? I thought witchery was inherited."

"Yes, but only from mother to daughter. I come from her son's side of the family, my great grandfather."

"Sons inherit nothing? No power at all?" I asked.

"One half," Dancing Star replied. "Unless is father is also a witch. If not, then his sons and daughters maybe inherit one fourth, and it gets less and less each generation; at least that's what they tell me."

I gave her another appreciative sidelong glance. "You're a real Foxy Lady. Aren't you afraid to get into cars with strange men?" I asked.

She looked at me and frowned. "Owl Woman protects me," she answered. "So don't get any ideas."

"What kind of ideas?" I asked feigning innocence.

"Oh, I see how you look at me," she said, opening her purse. "Do you want to see a picture of my boyfriend? He's on the football team. He could kick your butt!"

I glanced at the picture.

"Witches have world-wide organizations now," she said absently, her eyes on the photo. "They travel all over the world and have meetings, and form committees and fight injustice and male chauvinism which is really terrible here in Mexico."

"Do evil witches and good witches belong to the same organizations," I asked.

"No, evil witches have familiars, slaves, and they don't really get along with other witches, except when worshipping devils, and doing evil together."

"Do good witches ever do evil?" I asked.

"Yes! When she was young, like me, Owl Woman could conjure up ghosts and she would set them on other people if they made her mad or she didn't like them."

"Oh, and she has curse tablets made of copper and gold and its inscribed with spells and incantations. It's very old. Maybe she'll show it to you!"

"Cool," I replied.

Dancing Star sat up and pointed.

"You should slow down, there's a dirt road up ahead. It'll take us to her house."

We pulled up in front of an ancient adobe farmhouse, and parked between an old flatbed pickup truck and an equally old and dust covered 1940's Chevy sedan. I didn't see any crops or farm animals, other than a few chickens scratching in the dirt, and an old sow nursing its piglets beneath the porch. The old house needed a lot of work, paint peeling, cracked windows shuttered and draped. If not for the colorful and well tended garden, which I presumed wasn't just for growing flowers, one might suspect the old house was abandoned and no one lived here.

Before we got out of the car Dancing Star said to me: "The house is very old, dusty, and it always smells bad inside. That's why I brought cleaning supplies. Don't say I didn't warn you."

Dancing Star opened the rickety front door without knocking, and called out excitedly: "Madre! Abuela! Itotia Citali Te amo y está aquí para verte con un amigo!"

We entered a dimly lit living quarters illuminated with a greenish hue and were greeted by dozens of cats and a truly horrible odor: a mixture of cat shit, piss, incense, medicines, rotting flesh, and decay. Fragments of light streamed through the moth eaten heavy velvet curtains illuminating particles of dust suspended in the stagnant air.

It took a few moments for my eyes to adjust to the dark. The ceiling was water stained in patterns resembling clutching fingers. There were layers of dust, ropes of cobwebs, rickety wooden tables and mantles upon which sat old books, sepia photographs; and sealed inside glass jars things resembling big black spiders, snake heads, frogs' legs, bat wings and eyes of newt. Saucers containing burning candles and releasing twisting tendrils of smoke and stinky vapors curled the air. Old books, some open, lay upon the floor. Cats of all sizes and colors sat, rubbed against us, or chased dust balls across the old wooden floor which was marked with pentagrams and complex geometric designs.

And then I saw them: three incredibly old women; hags with long arms and nails, coarse hair, red eyes, and sharp and crooked teeth. One held a chicken's claw, another a goat's leg, the third a dark-haired Barbie-like doll over which they had been waving their free hands, chanting, and apparently casting a spell. The three hags looked up and smiled: but if these were signs of greeting, or they were thinking of eating us, was anyone's guess.

Dancing Star hugged each of them in turn, and exchanged words in a strange dialect I could not comprehend.

Dancing Star led me by the hand to a bedroom at the center of which was a crib-like basinet. The room was dark, shades drawn, the only light provided by flickering candles and sticks of incense releasing sickly perfumes. There were sepia-stained pictures on the wall, pots of flowers, some growing others wilting or dead, and saucers emitting smoke-like vapors. Assorted books were crammed every witch-way into wooden shelves. A human skull, crystals, and a large book lay open on an antique writing desk shoved into a corner, and all covered with cobwebs and dust. On the walls, more sepia photographs and faded and dust-covered paintings of Jesus and various Catholic Saints. The odor of death, decay, piss, feces, sickly vapors and medicinal perfumes, was almost overwhelming.

I followed Dancing Star to the basinet where she introduced me to Owl Woman: Ichhtaca Ihuicatl Tonalnan. Secret Sky Mother of Light.

"Owl Woman" lay skull-face up, sunken eyes closed, a few strands of long white hairs hanging from her otherwise bald and skull-like head. She was ghastly. Looked like putrefying yellow death. The shrunken bald headed ancient witch was about the size of a twisted, contorted, deformed anorexic seven year old with tissue thin blotched and wrinkled parchment for skin, her brittle bones and blood vessels visible just beneath the surface.

Dancing Star took her great great grandmother's withered, bony hand, kissed her on the forehead, and said something in a language I didn't understand.

Owl Woman opened her sunken eyes. They were clouded over. She was blind. She raised a gnarled claw-like hand, pointed at and motioned me closer. I complied. She opened her toothless mouth giving me a strong whiff of her mildewy and sickly breath. I fought the urge to recoil and gag. Speaking in a voice from beyond the grave, she uttered words unintelligible to my ears.

Dancing Star turned to me: "Owl Woman says she's been waiting for you. And now she can sleep."

"Waiting?" I asked in surprise.

"Yes. Owl woman says you are a warrior, a prophet, a dead man come back to life. She says you have lived and died many times in the past."

Again that voice from beyond the grave.

"Owl woman says, 'There is great danger. They will come!'"

"Who?" I asked.

In perfect Spanish Owl Woman answered: "La Trinidad. El padre les mostrará el camino."

"The priest of the trinity will show them!?" I asked.

"No," Dancing Star said, correcting me. "A priest. A trinity."

Owl Woman said more words in a dialect I didn't understand.

Dancing Star turned to me: "Owl Woman says he will cloak himself in darkness. Sophia she cannot see. The future can't be seen until its too late to change the past or the future."

I didn't understand anything Owl Woman was saying.

"Sophia is in darkness? What's that mean? That I can't find her?" I asked.

Owl woman croaked out more words which were unintelligible to my ears.

Dancing Star translated: "Owl woman says you must not search. You must see. Searching is not seeing. Looking is not seeing. See and you will find!"

"Did you tell her I was looking for don Rojas?" I asked.

Owl Woman closed her blind eyes and spoke at length.

Dancing Star translated: "Owl Woman says, 'search and a searcher you shall always be. Seek and you shall never find. The end of your journey is near. What you desire you will find without looking. You must see, not look. Follow the road with open eyes and you will see the path which will lead you to your desire.'"

"Can she tell me how to find don Rojas? Can she give me directions?" I asked.

Owl woman stirred yet again, and Dancing Star translated: "Beware. el hijo de Terranza."

Terranza? Isn't she dead?" I asked.

More unintelligible words, which Dancing Star repeated in English: "Evil follows you. He will show the way."

Evil follows me? "Is Owl Woman speaking about the Lt?" I asked. "Soldiers?"

Owl woman said nothing. She was so still, I wondered if she had died. And the odor in this nasty room already smelled like death. It was overpowering. I wanted to break open a window. The fragrance of cat piss, her rotting body and the sickening, medicinal vapors were staggering, stomach churning, mind-twisting, gut wrenching, leaving me feeling faint and dizzy.

Glancing at Dancing Star, I wondered: how can she stand it? Or, maybe she was a witch, after all.

The old woman began chanting, singing softly, and raised a gnarled bony hand, and made complex geometric motions. A smoke-like reflecting oblong circle of light appeared in mid air-- like a mirror-- and I could see, reflected, in the mirrored circle of light, me, the Lt, six others, in the jungle, creeping into the sleeping village, approaching the Shaman's hut which was painted with animal shapes and in complex mystical geometric designs and on the outside of which hung human skulls, shrunken human heads. A shot rang out. Man down. The Shaman angry, enraged, swung open the door to his hut, chanting and shouting curses, a man with a knife rushes toward me...

The old woman, chanting and singing struck the circle of light which spun like a mirror on an invisible string until finally coming to a halt.... inside the mirror: an upside down crucifix and the tortured face of Jesus becoming a moon-lit night... men, a man clocked in darkness, soldiers, weapons drawn... Three glowing entities beckoned... and... gun shots. The image disappeared.

The ancient old woman opened her blind eyes and spoke. Dancing Star translated her words: "Evil follows you. They will find him. Evil must be destroyed. Go back now, destroy evil, or all will be lost."

"Go back where?" I demanded. But Owl woman said no more.

7. The Door to Past Lives and Multiple Realities

Taking leave of Owl Woman and Dancing Star, I drove from Chinapa to Baroachi to Cananea stopping at each to inquire as to the whereabouts of don Rojas. Turned around and headed down to Banámichi, then up to Sinoquipe, then West on highway 15D for fifty miles then made a U-turn back to highway 89, stopping again and again to question the natives. All the while I was trying to "see" and not "look" for a familiar turn off which would take me to don Rojas and Sophia. Nada!

Honestly I had no idea what the difference was between looking vs seeing, and could not fathom how to search without searching. Questioning Dancing Star was met with a shrug of her lovely shoulders.

It was growing late, time to make camp and bed down for the night.

Chancing, completely by accident, upon a little road I'd first thought was a tree lined slope and gully, I turned right and maneuvered my VW down and over the rocky terrain. It was a hard-packed dirt road lined by an increasing number of scrub oaks and pines. A few minutes later I found a pleasant spot and made camp near the banks of the Rio Sonora, a grassy area dominated by forests of pine and oak.

Stripping down to shorts, tennis shoes, cowboy hat, and holstered gun, I jogged down then up the dirt road, thinking, turning over in my mind what Owl Woman and don Rojas had said about seeing vs looking, how I was not supposed to exist in this reality, and had lived past lives.

don Rojas said time was a circle, an an illusion, and that one's past and future life intersect, and all these lives live on in parallel dimensions, alternate realities, separate yet linked by the silver thread, past lives and future lives included!

Certainly I knew of and had read about reincarnation, had dreams of events, starring a version of yours truly, which seemed to have occurred in the past hundreds, thousands, tens of thousands of years ago; but dreams are not evidence of past lives.

don Rojas said it was a mystery why at age three I died, and still live. don Rojas' hinted I must have been spared for a reason. But what? Since childhood I've had this sense of purpose and a feeling that this reality is not real, that there is something hidden... and that I'm to do or discover something of great significance--and so I've sought to strip away the illusions, to rip away the veil which hides all, and to expand my mind, discover forbidden knowledge, and encounter the ultimate hidden reality. To touch the face of god!

The closest I'd come was LSD.

Fact is, my first LSD trip, back in 1967, was the most mind-expanding incredible experience I'd ever had in my life. Felt as if my intelligence had great expanded. I was seeing the world differently. Noticing what I'd never noticed before.

It was 1967, the summer of love when I first obtained this mind expanding miracle drug. Hippies, Hendrix, Led Zepplin, Jefferson Airplane, San Fransisco, Free Speech, Free Love, Flower Children, Mind Expansion, and LSD-- the "mind blowing" dangers of which had been wildly touted in newspapers, magazines and TV. From what I'd read, the key to the door to alternate realities was this magical little pill. And the place to get it was San Francisco's flower child hippie-land, at the cross roads of Haight and Asbury.

Lysergic acid diethylamide turned out to be everything the newspapers and politicians railed against: The key to mind expansion and stripping away the veil which conceals the ultimate reality.

My friends and I had taken my father's car to San Francisco to search out the maestro of psychedelics, Stanely Owsley, who'd been legally manufacturing LSD-25, and then continued after it had been outlawed, producing an additional 1.5 million doses, including "Purple Haze" --which Jimi Hendrix made famous when he sang: "Purple haze you're makin' me blow my mind... Excuse me, while I kiss the sky."

I and my friends, Richard, Jerod, Jerry and John, purchased five purple tablets, each guaranteed to contain over 1000 micrograms of pure LSD.

The plan: we'd take our "trip" to LSD never never land, in a safe and familiar environment: "The Park" back in the South Bay. This is where I dropped off my four good friends, each of whom--with the exception of John-- had consumed a fourth or half tab of this miracle mind-expanding drug during the drive home from San Francisco.

I parked my father's pontiac in my parent's garage, and then swallowed an entire tablet, 1000 micrograms. It was going to be my first trip on LSD.

As I walked the two miles to "The Park," trees, flowers, lawns, bushes became radiantly colorful as if illuminated by light from within. I took hold of a neon leaf, could taste the colors, could see the fine cellular structure then the green chlorophyl circulating through its veins...

By time I arrived at The Park, I was so overwhelmed with the multitude of vibrant changing colors, the optics, tastes, the aromas, the incredible vividity and clarity I sat down to take it all in. John, who'd declined to participate in our trip to other worlds, approached to see if I was alright. I couldn't speak, but grinned and waved my arm and hand only to see dozens of arms and hands trailing one after the other; each of which seemed equally real, as if there were numerous copies of "me" in parallel dimensions each waving their hand, albeit slightly out of sync with each other, and leaving ghostly trails in their wake.

I studied my hand. My eyes suddenly achieved the viewing power of a magnifying tunneling microscope--and this was 13 years before it was invented! I could see the fine cellular structure of the skin; and then, it was if my eyes had began tunneling beneath the skin. Cellular layers became apparent and the nuclei within... and then, I could see through the muscles, tend tendons, the bones of my hand, and was gazing at the Santa Cruz Mountains and Mount Umunhum with its WWII radar tower.

The mountain was no longer solid but punctuated by a streaming series of oblong holes which were in choo-choo train-like motion; rows and rows of holes flowing from left to right and popping in and out of existence, all going in the same direction--and I could see through these moving-holes, through the mountain to the other side... and my eyes became telescopic with tunneling vision, and before me: Monterey Bay, the Pacific ocean, waves crashing against the shore. And, I could hear a jet plane... and then I saw, through the holes in the mountain, a plane flying over the ocean, toward the mountains, and finally the plane appeared over the mountain, high in the sky; at which point John stepped in front of me, and said: "You've been staring at your hand for a long time."

I dropped my hand which became trails of numerous arms and fingers. I looked up at John and could see the waves and vibrations of his voice, the sound waves becoming optical and moving through the air toward me. John began to fractionate into billions of square-shaped particles, as if he was disintegrating and becoming a cloud of atoms and molecules; and I could see inside him: beneath his clothes, skin, muscle, tendons, blood vessels, skeleton, heart, lungs, his brain... and it seemed I could hear his thoughts, and then a jumble of thoughts as if I were hearing what Richard, Jerry, Jerod, were thinking....

... and then I could see right through him into the sky... and then the sky itself began to fractionate and split in half; and then, it was as if the sky was breaking apart and rolling away, in different directions, and I could see behind the sky: stars twinkling in the shimmering blackness of infinite night...

A veil had been stripped away....

There was incredible music, the sounds of a celestial symphony, and I could see gigantic, opaque, cloud-like-jellyfish swimming in the star-studded sea of space, hundreds of miles above Earth... and there were meteors, comets, and space-craft alien to my eyes... and then my mind telescoped and I saw a reddish rock-strewn desert planet populated only by a sea of purple mushrooms... and my eyes telescoped to the outskirts of the solar system which was ringed with the rubble of shattered moons and planets.... and then beyond into the blackness of starry night...

....and the heavens cleaved, broke apart and another veil of star studded darkness fell away... revealing a universe of mirroring reflections, reflecting reflections of moons, planets, stars, galaxies... for all eternity...

My eyes telescoped...and there was Earth... and another Earth... and another...

and another... spinning, orbiting, in hundreds of parallel mirror-like realities...

... and I could see me, dozens of me, some on LSD looking back at me in wonder, like a hall of mirrors, but each out of phase....

....and then these cosmic mirrors within mirrors reflecting reflections of infinite Earth, they shattered, and that veil too, fell away...

... I was gazing, now, into the grass beneath my feet... into the soil and there was a glow, a white light, growing brighter as my eyes penetrated through layers of rock and soil deep within the planet... and I realized the glow was a life force, radiating from a spinning moon-sized brain-like mass floating in a sea of molten metal, and Earth, our planet, is alive, conscious and watching us... ... and judging us...

...and then, that veil too, fell away...

And this was the first two hours of an increasingly fantastic, mind blowing, six hour "trip"--my first "journey" to parallel dimensions and alternate realities, courtesy of 1000 micrograms of LSD during the 1967 Summer of Love.

Unfortunately, all subsequent trips under LSD, did not come close to what I'd experienced the first time. Maybe it was because, what I later got my hands on, was not pure LSD. I still had the LSD tablets from the Institute, the ones manufactured by Sandoz--but had not yet had a chance to take any. I wish I had them now. I'd take two. But, alas, they were stowed safely at home back in the good 'ol USA.

On the other hand, the combined effects of the ingredients in those four satchels had propelled me to an alternate reality, unlike anything I dreamed was possible. Of course, it was not a positive experience. Really a bad trip. A bummer. And probably nothing more than a hallucination.

I still had doubts and wasn't sure if sorcery and witchcraft were real. And yet, I'd seen don Rojas and Owl Woman perform magic. Sure it could have been the power of suggestion, or maybe drugs in the vapors at the home of Owl Woman that somehow effected my mind. And yet, Owl woman had also given me a warning. I felt the threat was real.

I had a bad feeling. A sense of foreboding.

A swim in the Rio Sonora river did little to ease my troubled mind.

I tried to make sense of what Owl woman had said: someone was cloaked in darkness and this was related to the Trinity? Sophia can't see them? Sophia is in darkness? The future can't be seen and its too late to change the past? Evil will show the way? Evil must be destroyed. Go back now, destroy evil, or all will be lost.

What the hell had Owl Woman been babbling about? The only thing I could figure is she wanted me to kill someone.

I'd kill if I had to, and would enjoy doing it. There are a lot of men in need of killing. But how do I go back to destroy evil? Go back in the past? Or go to some location where I've already been? And what does any of this have to do with Terranza's son?

Maybe the old witch is senile. If not, then maybe she was urging me to kill the Lt. Certainly I didn't want him following me to the doorstep of don Rojas. But I'd seen no sign of those dudes since removing that tracking device. And what would killing him really accomplish? There were others where he came from.

Owl Woman said evil will show the way. Was Owl Woman referring to me? Is it me who will lead the way? No. I got rid of the tracking device. I've been watching the roads.

So who did Owl Woman want me to destroy?

Fuck it. I didn't come here to kill people.

The forest was growing dark. The creatures of the night were stirring. The three remaining satchels of magical herbs and plants, the doors and windows to other realities, parallel dimensions, lay within arm's reach. That's what I was here for! That and a $25,000 bounty.

Opening the satchel to door number five, I placed a pinch in the bone pipe, lit a match, and began to smoke. Twenty minutes later, other than cough cough coughing, it had no effect.

A cookie-like substance was inside magic door number six. Popped some in my mouth, gave it a thorough chew, swallowed it down with a Coca-Cola chaser. Hmmm. Nothing. Tried smoking, but it wouldn't stay lit; so I ate the rest of it.

I'm not crazy, certainly not a reckless drug addict, so I waited another 20 minutes before trying door number seven, the last satchel. The contents? A tough, thick, resiny flowery-vine with some kind of chalky sandy stuff mixed into the batch. Didn't look smokable or for eating, so, boiled some water, made a soup, let it cool, drank it down. Tasted like dead skunk! Gagging I grabbed a bottle of Coca Cola, intending to wash my mouth, when WHAM!

It was if I'd been blown high into the sky then slammed to the ground by the concussion of an exploding bomb. Stomach churning, mind spinning. Couldn't move. Flat on my back. Arms, legs pinioned to the ground. All I could do is lift my head and look at my stomach which was ballooning upward, outward, pulsating, growing larger. Something inside my gut was pounding, thumping against my stomach, like I was pregnant and about to give birth through my belly button to a hydra-headed alien that intended to crack me open like an egg and then run amok.

From my naval, beneath my shirt, something finger-like began to protrude, then there were more, pushing my shirt up and aside. Dozens, then hundreds of snake-like tubular tentacles, each consisting entirely of brilliant white light, emerged from my naval, growing longer, twisting and waving wildly in the air. The tips were ballooning outward then concave, each becoming like gigantic prismatic reflective spoon. They were like television screens, vividly remembering, depicting, and dreaming the dreams of different facets of my life, from birth to death, each gigantic prism providing different perspectives, as if viewed or remembered not only by myself, but unseen others.

And then.... I was seeing my future life, or rather, lives, each life different from the others, some vague and opaque, other vivid and real reflected in these spoon-like prisms erupting from my belly button... and I could see each of my future lives ending in death!

I saw myself die a hundred different ways, at different times, under myriad circumstances, as if gazing at multiple worlds each with their own reality, some more vivid than others, but each depicting an alternate death and the ending of this life lived by me... and the most vivid of all: I'm facing a phalanx of soldiers. They're shooting at me. I'm struck twice in the chest, topple to the ground, still breathing... the Lt walks up, stands over me, aims his gun at my head, pulls the trigger...

I'm dead...but not dead... my consciousness lives...I have only vague memories of who I am... who I was.... I'm lost in time... a spirit without a body swirling in a purgatory of empty space...ten years go by, then twenty, thirty, forty, fifty, sixty, seventy, eighty years in just seconds...

....I'm about to be reborn into a world ruled by women and the super-rich elite! A planet overrun by billions upon billions of autistic-like young men and women who sport wallet-sized-televisions-movie-theater-holographic apparatus which project movies, friends, relatives, real people in real time, right in front of them, by devices attached to belts, glasses, headbands and hats and who engage the wearer in conversations as if standing right there or next to them! Its remote viewing by electronics!

But I am not reborn... another soul has taken possession of the neonate at birth... and I drift... timeless, forgetting who I am, who I was, another ten years passes then another... its a hundred years into the future...The planet is in chaos... sea levels have risen over 100 feet... the entire East Coast of America, Florida, the Gulf states, San Francisco, the Bay Area, are under water....The glaciers are gone, the arctic is a vast sea, much of Europe, Japan, the Eastern and Southern coasts of Asia, India, all under water...

.....there is chaos, riots and mass murders as wave upon wave of impoverished and desperate men, women, babies, children, stream across the open borders seeking refuge and dry land, and killing all those who resist... its a planet wracked by wars, tornadoes, hurricanes, cyclones, profound droughts and temperatures in the 130s Fahrenheit! Disease, plagues, death, mass extinctions, rampant crime....

.... The planet is taking revenge and ridding itself of humanity which defiled their mother, the great god Earth... There are not enough new borns, bodies, be it plant, animal or human, for me to be reborn...

There is a flash of brilliant White Light.

I'm me, in this reality, and growing younger, as if watching a thousand movies of innumerable perspectives of my life in reverse... and all depicted on thousands of these spoon-like tentacles attached to and still emerging from my belly button, expanding, crowding together, merging, coalescing and enveloping my surroundings and body until all becomes a brilliant, glimmering, impossibly pure white light...

An entity, titanic, humanesque, shining bright, yet indistinct, appears within the pure light. It raise an appendage of silver light, strides forward, majestic, god-like, and shoves my head backwards, causing me to fall back back back through time. I am re-experiencing innumerable memories of past lives.

One hundred years into the past, two hundred years, three hundred, four hundred, five hundred, life after life...

... I am garbed in Dominican robes, teaching in Latin, Italian, and Greek:"...The soul is eternal and dwells in every living thing, even on other worlds just like our own!"

Followers, philosophers, Bishops, members of the Inquisition and Dominican priests, are gathered before me, some yelling "heretic" "witch" "warlock" and challenging my teachings and beliefs.

"The Bible says," a Bishop in anger yells, "Earth, not the sun is the center of the universe!" "Repent" a priest demands, "you know not what you say!" A representative of the Pope warns of arrest, torture and death: "Anathema! Blasphemy!" he says, "You have lost the one true way!"

"The sun is but one star in the infinity of night," I reply, "The stars, they too are suns, circled by planets like our own, and living beings, flowers, trees, the birds of the sky and fish which swim these far away seas, and beings like us, also dwell on these living planets which circle the stars which are suns not unlike our own."

"Heretic!" "Blasphemy!" "Epicurean!" they cry.

I am arrested, bound and led away. "Guilty" is the verdict of the Inquisitors. They beat me. I am tortured. An iron bar is pounded through my jaw to seal my lips for all time."Heretical" words I can no longer say. They bind and burn my living body, proclaiming as flames consume me, that: "hell fire and eternal damnation is thy fate."

And I fall back, further backwards through time, six hundred years, eight hundred, twelve hundred...flashes of distant memories, across the pages of past lives...

...I gaze wildly, excitedly through the eyes of a blood soaked Viking warrior priest, the leader of the tribe...there are screams and oaths of battle, men at war fight and die... wielding sword and broad ax I stab, slay, split heads, cut off arms, legs, shoulders, heads and hands... I cleave a man from crown to groin, another is sliced in half, his chest and head toppling over as hips and legs stand then fall. Sweating stinking yelling screaming blood stained fighting men are pressed against me, the trodden ground slippery with flesh, gore, and blood. I am exhilarated, exultant, euphoric and kill and kill again, my enemies falling at my feet and die... An arrow pierces my shoulder, a curve blade cuts through my side... I slay this foe...and then another... Victory will be ours, this new land shall soon be mine... Enemies let fly with arrows as they run away and hide...

A feathered arrow impales my throat, another, my chest. Mortally wounded, now gazing down from above, I have fallen in battle. Vikings gather sad and somber, none dare womanly weep... I am laid upon my shield and carried to a dragon-headed warship... there follows women, my wives and daughters crying, bearded comrades shouting oaths beating on their shields, grave goods, my weapons, prized possessions, and chained slaves... all to be sacrificed on my langskip funeral pyre to serve me in Valhalla, for on the field of battle as a mighty warrior I was slain.

And I fall back, back, further backwards through past lives... Fourteen hundred, sixteen hundred, seventeen hundred years, and so many lives...

I am a child, standing in the shallows of the Egyptian Alexandria sea, struggling against the current and sinking waters as the ocean recedes and disappears.... The ocean is gone! Ships and small boats lay helter skelter on their sides and sinking into the muck. There are crabs, giant shells and fish flopping on a sea of mud and the skeletal remains of ancient ship wrecks where moments before there had been crashing waves and a vast blue sea... I run across the wet sands where the ocean had been, picking up giant multi-colored shells some with wiggling living creatures still inside, and gazing in wonder at the buried treasures that moments before had been hidden beneath the sea... Men, boys, girls and women, run out onto the wet sand and muck picking up wiggling fish and laughing and talking in amazement because the ocean had receded back back back for miles and miles leaving the floor of the sea and all its wonders revealed for everyone to see.

Sailors, fishermen, sea-captains, and marines do not share our joy, but with puzzled, serious, even fearful looks abandon their stricken ships....and I hear yells and screams of men, women, children, sailors and marines, screaming, screaming, as they run toward the shore... and I hear a distant rumbling roar growing louder, coming closer, and looking up, there, in the far distance, a rushing WALL OF OCEAN. a MOUNTAIN OF WATER looming far into the sky... the ocean is returning, a titanic wave rushing toward where I am standing with sea shells in my hands. I run for my life, like everyone else, running running running...and I can see, over my shoulder, behind me, the roaring wall of ocean water coming closer, and closer... faster faster faster, then looming over now crashing down upon me, the salty sea filling my mouth and lungs and crushing the life from out of me...

And another life, and another...Eighteen hundred years, Nineteen hundred, two thousand... backwards through time...

.... I am a Galilean, a lustful violent man of thunder and fight, hailing from a village in Bethsaida, toiling as a fisherman, unhappy with wife, yearning for adventure, perhaps to abandon all and become a soldier, or sail the seas and live a pirate's life.. A tall handsome bearded man, a preacher, a prophet, approaches as I haul my fish to shore: "Follow me!" he says and promises riches, a kingdom, if for him and his god I war... He performs miracles, walks on water, heals the sick, gives sight to the blind, raises the dead, claims to be a god, and I believed then doubted for he loved women: Mary, Salome, many others who would cry and lovingly kiss his mouth and wash his feet, and he expected me to do the same on the last day of his life... the Romans, the Temple Priests, they killed him, when he said he couldn't die, and now he lay bloodied and dead, when he'd promised resurrection and ever lasting life... we stole his body from the grave and for three days prayed... but he only rotted and did not come back to life... and I said to my comrades: we must obey gods, not men.

And I am falling, back, back, backwards through time, another hundred, and another hundred years, reliving past lives...

... I am white haired and old, a scientist, astronomer, mathematician, an engineer of war, living and working in my castle tower in Syacuse the great city state. I've invented complex geometric formula, parabolas, spirals, cylinders, pumps, pulleys, and searched the cosmos with reflecting glass and copper spheres which magnify the stars which are planets and not gods. I've invented levers which can move the Earth, mechanical claws which seize and overturn enemy ships and send them to the bottom of the sea, and giant parabolic copper mirrors which reflect death rays and fire from the sun, setting aflame those Roman ships which besiege the city and which escaped the clutches of the claw. War rages outside the walls of Syracuse, and the Romans will soon overrun us all.

My books, On Floating Bodies, On the Equilibrium of Planes, On Spirals, On Conoids and Spheroids, The Quadrature of the Parabola, and On Sphere-Making which describes the movement of the Moon, Earth, and Sun, are studied by wisemen near and far... and now, as war rages, I am near to making an amazing discovery: a mathematical formula and a mechanical device which promises to unlock the secrets of the cosmos and the gods...

A helmeted Roman soldier, sword in hand, storms my chambers and places me under arrest, "by order of General Marcus Claudius Marcellus," and then scoops up my scientific and mathematical instruments as booty which he states, is now his to own by right of conquest.

In fury I rise and tear my instruments from his hands: "Fool! I am about to make my greatest discovery! I am not to be disturbed. The General and your greedy hands must wait," I shout. The soldier, enraged, stabs me to death with his sword.

....and I tumble backwards, round and round the circle of time, falling back, back, further back, five thousand years, ten thousand, twenty, thirty-five thousand years, remembering and reliving long ago lives...

I am human, a child, a creation, the ape-men say, of the Sky People, who are said to be demons and not gods, that descended from the heavens in great shining cloud-birds many moon-suns ago.

Clothed rudely in stinking, ill-fitting animals skins, I stand apart with my younger brothers and sisters. We've been taken captive by these creatures half-ape half-man and forced to adorn ourselves with these hairy-rags. I am gazing upon the body of Grok, as the ape-men lower and lay him in a deep hole dug with simple stone tools.

These ape-men-and-women, draped in filthy, stinking animals skins, are heavily muscled, much stronger and physically powerful than the "Sky People" who are slim and stand two, even three feet taller than the tallest ape-man. Already I am as tall as the ape-women, and unlike these half-apes, am pale white, with hair of gold, whereas the ape-men are brown and matted with clumps of hair as black as night.

They have little imagination, these creatures half ape half man and are as likely to grunt as speak in words. They are not creative or deep thinkers, for I can hear the thoughts in their heads. The tales they tell cannot be the stuff of dreams, but as real as the "shining bird-clouds" and "Sky People," who live in great dwellings which shine like the sun, guarded by "fire trees" and "devils" with spears of thunder and light. I know all this to be true for I was born and lived amongst the "Sky People" until three suns ago.

These ape-men think not of the future, or complex words or thoughts, except when it comes to death. To die is to sleep, and to awake and be reborn, among the gods.

Grok has been laid in a freshly dug pit, his body flexed, lying on his side as if in sleep, with a flat rock as a pillow, because, the ape-men believe, "Grok not dead" "Grok go to spirit world" of gods and dreams. It is while dreaming, the ape-men believe, that one's soul may transcend the body, to soar like an eagle, to commune with the spirits and loved ones who reside in heaven along side the stars and gods, who, in dreams, make their intentions known.

The ape men and women toss food and blooming, blossoming, fragrant flowers upon Grok's dead body now sleeping in a man-sized hole. They sing and dance, and in their simple speech recount the great deeds of Grok, as they cover his grave with earth. Now buried, the women place goat horns in a circle to mark his final resting place.

And now they recount the legends, of Grok, my father-who-is-not-but-is: The Sky People from heaven descended in sky birds shaped like silver clouds. They are giants, with silver hair and skin, two heads taller than Grok who was the tallest among the tribes and the men.

The Sky People searched out the ape-men who with wives and children hid. The Sky People said they are "Sky Gods from the heavens" and have come to "Gaia" to stay, and offered much good food and drink, asking who was the wisest among the clans. These wisemen and women the Sky People took to their silver clouds, great dwellings of magic and power. Over many moons the Sky People taught Grok and the wisest of the few, words to speak, plants to water and grow, to care for vast gardens and forests of fruit bearing trees, to tend to bisons and other animals guarded with tall spears of flame and fire and which are the divine food which only the god's alone may eat.

And the Sky People taught: "Thou shalt not kill." "Thou shall not steal." "Thou shall not eat of the animals or the fruit bearing trees, for these are the possessions of the gods." "Thou shall obey the gods or suffer grievous injury and death." To disobey is a sin." "Disobey and thou may die."

Grok, and those chosen by the Sky People, did not wish to obey, and were not afraid to die. "What is sin?" Grok asked, and he and his wives ate the animals and the fruit of the forbidden trees.

"Thou shalt not steal," the Sky People had taught. But Grok had said, the fruit is good to eat, and Grok did not die. So Grok disobeyed the gods, and he and the others killed the animals and ate the fruit of the trees. And for this sin, Grok and his men, were punished and driven away, outside the fire trees which guarded all within. But of the wisest of the ape women, these were made captive, and of these women, I, and my younger sisters and brothers were born.

Grok was angry, desired vengeance. Grok wanted back his wives and the children they bore. The Sky People, Grok had said, and showing the now healed wound upon his ribs and chest, had wanted to steal Grok's soul while he slept. And now the Sky People had stolen Grok's women and wives.

"What is sin?" Grok had asked of the tribes. "Thou shall not steal?" "From Grok the Sky People steal!" Grok angrily yelled, pounding on his massive muscular chest.

For many moon-suns--they ape-men said as they stood over his grave--Grok had sought revenge and to take back what is Grok's. But the white clouds where dwelled the Sky People, and their gardens, animals, fruiting trees, were guarded by fire-trees and spears of fire which kill those who dare to touch.

After many sun-moons, Grok dreamed and saw a way. It was in the darkness of a moonless night, when Grok and his warrior-ape-men chopped a fire tree down, then attacked and killed many Sky People who with false tongue had said they were gods who could not die. Grok stole back his woman and the children she had bred; and I, my sisters and brothers, were overpowered. Not strong enough to resist, we were carried away by these ape-men and who gave us animals skins to wear and dress.

And all the clans, that night, ran far to the North, and to the West where in caves deep and wide they hid.

For two suns the Sky People searched for Grok and my sisters, brothers, and I. But we'd been hidden away in deep caves beyond the sight of eye. But Grok they found and severely punished, then killed because Grok had sinned and broke the law: "Thou shall not steal." "Thou shall not kill." Now Grok, the great leader, was dead.

But as the half-apes sang and danced around the grave where Grok slept and dreamed, the Sky Birds and Silver Clouds had found and were hovering overhead.

"They come!" the ape-men said too late, for with silver bodies glowing, the

Sky People surrounded us on all sides, their silver spears belching fire and ice and many ape-men died.

...And then the dream-like memory of this past life began to fade...

A brilliant white light surrounds me, an entity, shining bright, stands before me and touches my head. There is a brilliant flash and I am enveloped in a glowing endless sea of incredibly pure white light.

I am me, this is now. In the forest. My campsite. I'm sitting up, can't move, submerged in a sea of white... and in the ocean of light there is a chaos of overlapping faint shadowy silhouettes resembling cars, chairs, walls, lamps, buildings, trees, ships, and animal- and human-like entities juxtaposed within, without, on top of, inside of, above, below, and in positions and locations in defiance of the four dimensions and laws of gravity. I didn't know if I was hallucinating or gazing into another world, an alternate reality, a parallel dimension completely unlike our own.

I felt as if watery waves of electricity were pulsating in flowing repeating patterns of tingling motion, up my body, to my head from my toes, wave after wave increasing in frequency, intensity, electric-like-power and energy flowing up and down my body...

"It is he!" said a voice, deep inside my head. And there, levitating before me, glowing in an endless sea of the purest white, a Trinity, three entities in shadowy humanesque silhouette. They were without color other than radiating an intensity that superimposed their existence upon the all surrounding white upon white.

Two entities were several feet apart, levitating, facing each other, and the third, standing between the two, was facing directly my way. They seemed to be conversing, deep in conversation and thought--totally unaware of my existence. All around them things and objects were moving and flowing in juxtaposed overlapping and shadowy silhouettes.

"Wow. Far out!" I thought."

The entity in the middle, as if having heard my inner voice, looked in my direction then slowly raised an arm-like appendage, pointing directly at me. The two entities on its either side, turned their head-like visages, as if noticing me for the first time.

All three, now pointing, took a step toward me, then another.

I realized this could be a hallucination, but also remembered what don Rojas taught about the dangers of entering alternate dimensions. It seemed these three were coming for me. No, I didn't like this at all.

"Oh ye of little faith," said a voice inside my head.

They held out what I perceived to be arms and hands, and I heard three voices in my head which became one:

"I am Alpha and Omega, the beginning and the end. I am the resurrection, and infinite eternal life. He that dares to see within shall gain infinite wisdom and shall live forever and never die."

"Come with us," they said, inside my head: "Eat of the fruit of knowledge and never hunger or thirst again. Drink of the sea of knowledge and live eternal life in this and other worlds. For whoever wants to save their life will lose it, but whoever devotes their life to wisdom will save it. What good is it to gain the whole world, when there are so many other worlds to gain. Do not live in the darkness of ignorance and forfeit the soul! There is no sin. Be afraid not to throw stones. Assail the gatekeepers, for they are graves that appear not. Assail the sacred towers for they are tombstones that appear not. Topple and shatter the fallen idols worshipped by the temple priests of science who cannot see and hear not."

"Only those with eyes may see. Let those with ears, hear. Worry not about tomorrow, for tomorrow is the past. Time is a circle, and those who seek to be first, will be last, and those who are last will be first only to be crushed by the wheels of time. That which is born of the flesh is flesh: and that which is born of the gods, becomes Spirit and lives eternal life in not just this world, but all worlds which are infinite and without number and become one which is God. Doors lead to doors, open one and then another, mirrors reflecting mirrors, dimensions within dimensions. Where will it end? Only the gods may know."

The three entities took another step toward me, their arms open wide over their heads, hands touching hands, forming a circle which was transformed into double arched rainbows, a gateway shimmering within the sea of pure light.

"Enter these doors and gain cosmic wisdom, and eternal life, for the knowing soul shall never die but will live again on many worlds and become one with the all knowing All. Listen, for your hour is coming. Even those dead in their graves may hear this voice--but only if they have ears that hear and eyes that see. They shall be reborn from darkness into the infinite light of wisdom, and those who harken to the voice of the gods, will be rewarded with the eternal resurrection of life and knowledge possessed by all the gods and enter the gateway that leads to all worlds and then behold All. Blessed are the pure in heart with eyes that see: for they shall see God, become God, and achieve cosmic wisdom, a unity with the oneness that is All."

"Consider the lilies of the field, how they grow; they toil not, neither do they spin. They live in the eternal now for they have learned to see."

"Seek and ye shall not find. Search and a searcher thy shall always be. The kingdom of knowledge is within you, all around you, is you, is All, a light shining bright, daring to illuminate the darkness which is man's mind. A man of knowledge becomes the light of the world, of all worlds, but only if he embrace the cosmic light."

They took another step toward me, arms beckoning, the double door arched rainbow gateway between them, behind them, above them, below.

They were approaching me, getting closer, and I was beset by a tempting thought: Get away from them. Escape. Do it now. And yet, I remembered: do not take counsel of your doubts. Never give up. Courage shall conquer fear.

Another step, the rainbow gateway before me.

"Enter ye in into the doorways of heaven, for wide is the gate, and broad is the way, if though wishes to be a man of knowledge. For all knowledge, alpha and omega, the beginning and the end, to see all things in the future and the past, in other worlds, and realities, the infinite cosmos with the eye of god, all is within your grasp."

The double arched rainbow doors opened and I could see darkness and pearls of light swirling and spiraling inside.

"Come. Enter. And become one with the eyes of gods."

Another step toward me. Closer. Arms reaching. They weren't inviting me. They were going to take me--or maybe take my soul leaving an empty vessels behind.

I drew back, feeling fear. A competing thought: Never surrender. Never retreat. Do not take counsel of your fears and doubts. But there's a difference between retreating and being taken captive never to return!

I remembered what don Rojas taught about the silver thread. Demons and devils can steal and possess your body. Even sorcerers who dared to enter these alternate realities, parallel dimensions, could become slaves.

"Come with us and live forever," they said inside my head, "and become one with cosmic wisdom and the god which is one, the unity of all."

I was convinced if I let them grab me, if I stepped through those rainbow doors, I would not live forever, but die forever and never return to this reality again.

"No thanks!" I said aloud.

They came closer. Beckoning me to enter. They were right before me.

"The kingdom of knowledge is come unto you and he that enters here will attain the eternal wisdom of the cosmos, the infinite knowledge of the gods. You shall see as Gods. You shall be as gods and become one with the infinite. The doors are before you who has been chosen. Enter!" the entities commanded.

They reached down and took hold of my wrists, my skin burning at their touch.

But I recoiled in a panic, shouting: "Fuck this! Hallucination or not, I'm getting the hell out of here."

Jumping up, I turned and ran for my life into the blinding surrounding pure light, only to smash my head and chest against something hard. Stunned, I collapsed, my head throbbing in pain... and then, the flickering light of consciousness was extinguished and the pain went away... My mind was floating in air and could see me, down below, lying on the ground, on the forest floor, crumpled next to a tree... and I looked dead...

Then, this sense of consciousness rose higher into the air, and down below I could see the smoldering remnants of the campfire, the sleeping bag, satchels, coke bottles, leaves, branches, the detritus of the forest floor, more trees, and my body lying still, unmoving, looking dead...

... and that fragment of consciousness rose higher still, above the trees, then higher still, and I could see highway, the turnoff I'd chanced upon, my car, camp-site, me, laying on the ground, and up ahead, a paved road, and in the far distance, a bridge, and don Rojas' hacienda on the other side.

8. Seeing vs Looking, Multiple Futures, Parallel Dimensions, Magic is Technology

Somewhere, far off, deep in my mind, aroused by throbbing pain, flickers of consciousness became a dull, gradual drowsy wakefulness, coupled with a full blown massive headache. My eyes opened. I was lying on my back, next to a tree, the surroundings illuminated by remnants of the camp fire and the rising of the dawn sun.

The bump on my forehead was painful to the touch. My chest was bruised. I must have slammed into a tree when making my escape from those three entities. Yes, the tree was real. The pain was proof of that. But the three entities?

As near as I could figure, it was all a horrific hallucination, or, somehow I must have passed over to another dimension, and appeared in an alternate reality; and those three entities were as surprised to see me, as I was to see them. As to the "Alpha and Omega" stuff? I didn't know what to make of that, but decided, once my headache began to pass, I'd write it all down and puzzle over it later.

Of one thing I was sure: I knew, in my heart, I had accidentally found the turn off and camped along the road that led to don Rojas' palatial hacienda. As to the three entities? Hallucination or not: Total bummer. A bad trip.

Two hours later, after a swim in the river, and still nursing a headache, I crossed the bridge leading to the ranchero, and drove past fields and crops tended by laborers, some of whom ceased working, and looked up and stared zombie-like or in a manner reminiscent of goats, horses, and cows. Up ahead, nearly hidden by trees, the magnificent castle-like hacienda, with flowing fountains, a wide circular brick driveway and jeeps and pickup trucks parked out front.

Seven men, five of them with big smiles, came loping toward me as I pulled up and were now walking back and forth on both sides of my car, smiling, or just staring at me, but saying not a word. Their manner reminded me of friendly and not so friendly dogs.

don Rojas, his face a smile, accompanied by two young, slim, female servants, emerged from the hacienda. The seven men bounded toward him, the female servants arching cat-like and stepping back. With a clap of don Rojas' hands, and giving a whistle, the men stopped, turned away, and went back to laboring on their assigned tasks.

After exchanging greetings, and examining the bruise on my forehead, don

Rojas took me by the arm and led me through the stained glass double door entrance of the big hacienda, asking many questions. The two female servants followed, almost cat-like, in their slinky movements, but said nothing.

The old lady housekeeper made an appearance, and don Rojas instructed her to prepare a bedroom for yours truly, an elixir for my headache, and lunch for two.

"Only two?" I asked innocently. "Sophia won't be joining us?"

don Rojas laughed, and patted my shoulder affectionately. "My love-sick gringo amigo, you will never learn."

"I believe I've learned a lot since we spoke last," I replied as we entered the dining room.

"And when was that?" he asked, giving me a whimsical smile.

The two very feminine female servants took cushioned seats far from the table, curled their legs beneath them and watched with disinterested oriental-eyes.

"Your two servants, are they Asians?" I inquired.

"Why do you ask?"

"Their eyes, slinky movements. There's something inscrutable about their demeanor...which reminds me of Orientals ...and, I don't know why exactly, but cats!" I answered.

"Gatito gatos!" don Rojas said with a laugh. "Aquí gatito gatito. Kitty cat!" he said, smiling at them both.

"Meoww" they both mewed.

I laughed. "Very cute!"

I wondered if these two Oriental girls were also servants in his bedroom.

"What do they do, other than meow?" I asked teasingly.

"Do? What does any cat do? Nothing!" don Rojas answered. "They are pets, my amigo gringo. Mascotas. Nothing else."

Lunch served. We ate, talked, he asked questions and listened. The food was delicious and the elixir completely washed away my aches and pain.

"Where's your daughter?" I asked.

"Paciencia, my amigo! Sophia will be back before evening," don Rojas answered with a smile. "She is paying respects."

"Respects?"

"Mujer Búho. Owl Woman: Ichhtaca Ihuicatl Tonalnan. She died late last night, after you left her home," don Rojas answered.

"Wow! I'm sorry," I replied.

don Rojas laughed: "Even when I was young Owl Woman was old. Owl Woman had a good long life. It was her time to die. She will live again, in another life. Nothing to be sorry for."

"How'd you know I was at her place?" I asked.

"Owl Woman came to me in a dream, a vision, to say goodbye and showed me of your visit."

"Did she tell you what we talked about?" I asked.

"No. Owl Woman did not speak. Her soul appeared in a dream. Now tell me everything she said to you."

"It was mostly jiberish," I replied. "A jumble of words and phrases."

"I am listening," don Rojas said.

So, I told him almost word for word, and then asked: "Is Terranza's son, a danger to you?"

don Rojas smiled ruefully. "No. He is but a black priest, has little power."

"A priest?" I asked. "He's a negro?"

"A black priest to the diablo. Worships el demonio. He is Maldito. Cursed. Estar como una cabra. Loco! Malacopa. He poses no threat to us. Do not concern yourself with this naco cholo," don Rojas replied dismissively.

Lunch consumed, don Rojas led me to the East wing where we passed several massive arched doors, all closed and bolted.

"What's in these rooms?" I asked.

don Rojas smiled and said: "Magico."

"Why the bolts and locks?" I asked.

"la curiosidad mató al gato," he answered. "The spirit helpers, los lobos and el gatos, they are curious, Si? Even I tell them, 'no go inside,' the curiosity may kill the cat. Magic can kill."

"I saw myself die, and being killed," I said. "Hundreds of times." I proceeded to tell don Rojas what happened, the hallucinations of past lives, after consuming the last three of the seven keys to other realities.

"First I fell forward into my future," I explained. "Or rather, I should say 'futures' because there were hundreds of them, each increasingly different from the others, and with me dying at different ages and under different circumstances. I really didn't care to see all that."

"Si! Watching oneself's die so many ways, can be upsetting. Si."

What I didn't tell don Rojas is I also saw myself lying on the brick driveway of the hacienda, two bullets in my chest, and the last bullet, fired point blank into my head.

"I don't believe I saw my future," I added. "It was just a very interesting and disturbing hallucination."

"I think you are wrong," don Rojas said.

"But I saw hundreds of different futures! How could I have more than one future?"

"Choices. The different futures, they exist in different realities, parallel dimensions. You chose your future. Si. Many choices. Many futures. Different choice futuro diferente," he answered. "This is why it is difficult, even for a man of knowledge to see the future. There are too many."

"I don't understand," I said.

"The future is like the weather which always changes. Easy to say what weather will be today. What it will be next week? Here? There? In New York? Ciudad de México? No one knows. Many futures, many choices. Choices change to a different future, like the wind changes the weather to a different weather."

"How can more than one future exist, and yet change?" I asked.

"You change which future you chose, like change the channel of the television. Think of the tree with its many roots," don Rojas explained. "Each root can be a choice which leads to un futuro diferente."

"If that's true, then why'd they differ in visual intensity?" I asked. "When I consumed that stuff in the last three satchels, some of these visions of my future lives and deaths were faint, opaque, ghost-like and ended quickly. Others were extremely vivid and ended quickly or went on and on until I was very old."

don Rojas explained: "Probabilidad matemática! What choice is most likely? High probability you make choice to marry smart beautiful woman. Low probability you marry estúpida un feo, ugly woman. One choice probabilidad alta, other choice not likely. Each choice, different future with strong or weak probability."

"Think of the leaf which falls into the river and makes the small ripples in the water. Pequeñas ondulaciones en el agua. This can be the small choice, or the choice you probably do not make, and it has poco impacto, little impact on the river of life. Now a tree falls into the river and makes the big splash and many waves that last long time and make mucho splash on the shore. The leaf is small choice not likely you make, the tree is the big choice most likely you make, and each choice, each decision, cada decisión, makes the ripples that determine the future life. If you marry a woman you love or she rejects you and marries another hombre, your life will be different, Si? Las elecciones determinan el futuro! Choices effects the river of life, and each future exists in the future, some more probable than the others. Algunos más probables que otros."

"What do you mean, 'they exist'? All these futures actually exist? How is that possible?" I asked.

"Todos los caminos conducen a Roma," don Rojas answered.

"What's that roads to Rome got to do with it?" I asked.

"El futuro tiene una ubicación y está en un lugar, que existe en el espacio," he replied.

"What?" I asked.

"The future is a location, a place, and a destination; like a city you wish to visit. There are many cities. Many roads to get there. All roads lead to Rome. You chose to go to Rome which exists in your future until you get there, then it becomes the present. The Now," he answered.

"Sorry. I don't get it," I admitted. "And what's this got to do with Rome?"

don Rojas explained: "Rome exists. Si? All the roads to Rome exist. Si? Take one road, and all the other highways, las otras carreteras, still exist even though you no take. The road you do not take, it grows weeds, trees, bushes, and disappears. But Rome still exists. If you go to New York instead, Rome exists. Aún existe! Rome, the roads, they exist before you begin your journey no matter what city you visit, Si? Think of Rome not as a city, but a location in one of your futures. There are many cities, many futures. Many roads many choices, some high probability, some not so. You decided to what city and which road you wish to travel. But Rome always exists, even you do not go there. The same is true about the future."

"If the future already exists, is that why some people have premonitions about the future?" I asked.

"Si. Premonitions?" don Rojas replied. The big tree falls in the river, and the ripples from the future reach you before the tree flows by. This is why, some know what is to happen, before it happens. They feel the waves and ripples from the future that already exists."

"If there is more than one future, then how can one perceive the future just before it happens?" I asked.

"The big tree makes the big ripples; but sometimes, other choices you make, and this is why, only sometimes you may know the future and others times, you do not; because it changes just before it becomes the now," don Rojas explained.

"Sorry, I still don't understand how there can be more than one future," I said.

"Which future you live, is determined by which road you chose to take. Each road is different, leads to different choices, many side roads, stores, places to go. Take the wrong road, decide to go somewhere else at the last minute, the hacienda still exists, even if you never find it. There are many futures. All exist, each in their own separate reality. Dimensións paralela. You chose your future, your destiny," he explained. "And the future most likely to be chosen, may change to another future at the very last moment, because of choices you make, or the choices others make."

"Can a sorcerer go back into the past, make a different choice, and change the future?" I asked.

"The choice determines which future is chosen," don Rojas answered. "And the future which is chosen, has many roads leading to many futures."

"Sophia sent me into the past, twice," I said. "Did she do that so I'd make different choices? Or was this some kind of female game and she was just messin' with my head?"

"Dos veces?" don Rojas rubbed his chin thoughtfully. "We must ask her."

"Can Sophia see the future? Can you?" I asked.

"Me? Sólo unos pocos minutos. Only a few minutes," he answered. "Sophia, she has the gift, but she can only see one day, maybe two days into future time. The future is hard to see," he said, "because there are so many, and all change, like the weather."

"If Sophia was trying to change the future, then the result was I killed eight men."

"Tell me what happened," don Rojos asked, and then listened patiently, saying nothing.

When I finished telling don Rojas about killing those eight bandits, I was careful to say nothing about Snake Eyes. Nor was I going to tell The Company about don Rojas. I'd forgo the $25,000. Instead, I'd provide a blank log book, and report failure. Fuck The Company.

"Did you kill with sorrow in your heart?" don Rojas asked.

"No. I enjoyed it. It was a rush. They deserved to die."

"You destroyed evil. That is good. And the two women?" he asked.

"Dead," I answered.

don Rojas didn't ask for details.

"Anyway, after seeing myself die a thousand different ways, I fell back in time, and began having dream-like hallucinations of past lives."

"Why do you believe they were not real?" he asked.

"I have my reasons. For one, it doesn't make sense, scientifically."

"You are wrong, my amigo. To die and live again is the nature of the soul. One cannot destroy the soul which is energy. The soul, energy, power, can only become a body, physical, matter, or it becomes energy, soul. The soul gives life to matter, the body. Come with me."

At the center of the castle-like hacienda, we entered a palatial great hall, two stories tall, of native and exotic woods, smelling strongly of flowers and incense, and adorned with balustrades hand-carved from single pieces of white marble. There were dreamy frescoes of angels, clouds and Aztec, Mayan, and Toltec gods on the upper walls leading all the way to the ceiling which was topped with a massive, intrinsically detailed, domed gilded skylight. The skylight was beautiful, unique, and ribbed with panels of stained glass and mirrors reflecting and allowing both direct and indirect sunlight to illuminate everything within, including a fragrant, blossoming, indoor garden.

"Wow," I said, taking in the surroundings.

Exquisite masterful Aztec murals, codices, and statues and artwork of gold and jade were also set against or adorned the walls of the first floor, one of which, facing the courtyard, was dominated by a huge multi-paned-stained glass window depicting colorful scenes from ancient Mexico and topped with smaller panes depicting stars, planets, moons, galaxies, and the Aztec sun god. On yet another wall were paintings of Toltec and Mayan cities, pyramids and astronomical observatories; paintings which to my untrained eye, appeared to be antediluvian and to predate the conquest of Mexico by Cortez. They were incredibly beautiful, awesome to behold.

don Rojas led me to an intricately designed glass case, containing numerous skulls, skull-art, crystal skulls, jade and ebony snakes, and obsidian mirrors which, he said, had been hand-crafted by Mayan, Toltec, and Aztec sorcerer priests. don Rojas removed one of the skulls and placed it in my hands. There were an assemblage of crystals embedded in the eye sockets which flashed and gleamed in the indirect light of the sun.

"These skulls are from before the Conquest and destruction of the Aztec empire," he explained. "They are very old, from the time of the Toltec and Mayas. They have much power, magic."

"How's that?"

"These are the skulls of great Toltec and Mayan sorcerers. The skulls, they were worshipped by the Aztec emperors, priests, and the people. Before the Conquest, skulls were also carved from rock, obsidian, jade, and crystals which have much power."

I handed the skull back to don Rojas and asked: "What kind of power?"

"Think of a television. It is made of glass, electrónica, tecnología. A conquistador, if he saw the television, would think: mágico! But it is not magic. It is tecnología, a source of information, which is power. Some crystal skulls are not mágico. They are tecnología from the ancient past. To look into the crystal skull, into the crystal eyes, one might see into distant lands, to search for enemies, those you love, and to look into the past."

"Okay, if you say so," I replied.

From the glass case don Rojas handed me a skull made entirely of an assemblage of crystals.

"Look into the eyes of the crystal skull," he said, "and hold it to the sunlight."

I did as instructed. The crystal eyes became illuminated and seemed to gaze into my own. My hands and fingers began to tingle, as if exposed to mild bursts of static electricity. The entire crystal skull began to sparkle and shine with inner illumination whereas the crystal eyes filled with an aurora of swirling clouds of cerulean and glaucus light... and then, within the eyes of the crystal I could see a mournful procession of old women and men, and Dancing Star, walking solemnly behind a coffin which was carried on the shoulders of grim-faced men. Damn she was a good looking babe! I would have loved to pull her panties down! And there was Sophia, beautiful Sophia, dressed in back, and walking at the end of the procession. She looked up at me, frowned and flicked her fan... her image disappeared in a swirl of milky clouds of reds blues and greens... and then, there was Snake Eyes who was squinting right at me.

"Fuckin A!" I said, startled. I handed the crystal skull to don Rojas. "How'd you do that?"

"Tecnología. Not magic," he answered.

"What kind of technology? How can it see things far away? Where does it get the energy to make it work?"

"The crystals, each are chosen for their properties, and then the crystals are diseñado, engineered together to make the skull work like the computadora IBM," he said.

"An IBM computer?" I asked, interrupting. "Those things are huge, the size of a refrigerator."

"The crystals are like a computer, many very small computers, pequeño, very tiny. The power is from your body, and the sun. It looks into your eyes and sees what is in your brain. The eyes are the window to the soul, alma. The sun it sees everything. The crystals combine and see, like the television."

Was this how Sophia was able to track me, watch me, the find me when those witches almost carried me off to hell?

He put the crystal skull back in the glass case and said: "I have here, my amigo, many different skulls, some carved of stone and jade. Others are the skulls of the powerful sorcerers who long ago lived and died."

"But why choose a skull to be a computer? What's so special about a skull? Because they once held the brains of sorcerers?" I asked.

"Si. The Aztecs, Toltecs, Mayas believed the skulls are a symbol of death, but also life, resurrection, to live again. Rebirth from a past life, to another life. Do you think your mind, your soul lives in your feet? The mind is in the head, the skull."

"Why not worship the brain, instead?" I asked.

"It rots," he answered. "The flowers, herbs inside one of the satchels you mixed with water and drank as a soup were sprinkled with bone dust from a sorcerer's skull. This is why you traveled back in time to your past lives."

"How's that possible?" I asked.

"By unlocking the memories locked in your brain. In your DNA. Genetics. Genetic Memories. Not magic. Chemical tecnología. Alcohol make the brain drunk. The bone dust effects the brain, and make you see the past lives and the future, rebirth."

From the glass case don Rojas handed me an obsidian mirror.

"Many of these mirrors are carved from obsidian, jade and imanes," he said. "They have mucho power."

"Such as?" I asked.

"To lift into the air and move the huge blocks of stone," he answered.

"One mirror can do that? How?"

"Not one, but many, they reflect to each other back and forth, and harness the power of imanes, magnetismo, and the sun. The magnetismo and light grows stronger when reflected to and from many mirrors. The reflections reflecting the power of the sun and the imanes, increase and release much power."

"You're saying that mirrors, magnets and the sun can move buildings?" I asked.

"Si! And mucho more. Make fire. Even cut and melt the stone. Look into the mirror," he said.

"If I do, will it set me on fire? Maybe lift me in the air?"

"No. This mirror is not magnetismo. It was used by Mayan, Toltec, and Aztec sorcerers and priests in rituals to look into the underworld, to communicate with the realm of the dead. And the dead may be you, from a past life. Or your death in this life."

I looked into the mirror. My reflection was cloudy, distorted, then the clouds seemed to blow away. I saw a reflection of me, lying on the ground, bullet wounds in my head and chest... and then the image disappeared as if swallowed by ripples of water... now the mirror was reflecting me sitting on the ground, weeping, crying... and then as if swallowed by ripples of water that image too, disappeared, and I was in my car, at the Pemex gas station staring at the wind shield...Then, I was standing before a tribunal of angry, shouting generals, threatening me with death...

I handed the mirror back to don Rojas. I didn't like these futures at all and had no desire to see more.

don Rojas invited me to join him on a stroll about the ranchero.

As we walked, I could not help but notice the odd mannerisms of the laborers. Couldn't put my finger on it, but, the workers, their body movements, attitudes, reminded me of goats, rabbits, mice, birds, and dogs.

He led me to his beautiful gardens of herbs, spices, tomatoes, and magical plants, and every so often would get down on his knees to examine leaves and soil.

"I don't understand how one can see, without looking." I said.

"And yet, my Gringo Amigo," he answered without looking up, "you found the path to the ranchero when you were not looking. Si?"

"Yes," I admitted. "But how?"

"Because you were not looking. You freed your mind and your mind saw the road and remembered," he said.

don Rojas led me to a plot with purple plants and said, as he inspected the soil: "My amigo, have you sometimes had problem, problemas para recordar, remembering a word, or a name, when you speak? una palabra o un nombre?" don Rojas asked, "The forgotten word that is on the tip of the tongue?"

"Yes," I replied.

don Rojas looked up at me and said: "When the word is on the tip of the tongue, you know the word, but can't find it. Si? What you know is hidden from you, even though you know it is there. Si?"

"Yes," I agreed.

"You search your mind, your memory, tu memoria, to find the word. You give up, stop looking. Si? Then, como magia! You remember the missing word. Search and look you cannot find. No more look, and you see the word in the mind. This is seeing without looking, without searching."

"This same principio: can't find the car keys. Look everywhere, keep searching. Give up. Stop looking, then, como magia! There are the keys, where they have always been: right before your eyes. This is seeing without looking," don Rojas explained.

"Sorry. How that can apply to hidden wisdom, or seeing other dimensions," I asked.

"By freeing the mind. By not thinking in words. By using the senses we have been taught to ignore," he answered.

"What senses?" I asked.

"The dogs smell odors we cannot. Si? The birds they return home for the winter, but how they find their way, we know not. Bats, fish, whales in the sea perceive what most hombres cannot. Much of the world is hidden from humans."

"Yes, hidden, but why?" I asked.

"The psychiatrist say those who see or hear what others cannot, are crazy, loco, el psiquiatra dice que están locos. The doctors put those who see in the hospital, manicomio, and give the drugs to put the mind to sleep. Children are taught not to believe what they see if they see what their parents cannot. Windows they close. The doors, they lock."

"The mind has been put to sleep, and cannot see because it can't believe and lives in a box with no windows or doors. The people are taught not to see, and do not want to see, because they do not want to be loco. They are afraid to see and then, can no longer see. No use muscle, then lose muscle. If you wish to see without looking you must unlock your mind, find the windows and the doors, and stop ignoring what is right before your eyes: then you can see."

"And peyote, mushrooms, magical plants, can do this?" I asked.

"They only open the doors, in your brain, tu cerebro, which are locked," he answered.

don Rojas gathered a bulbous purple plant from his garden and placed it in my hands.

"This plant, you chew, then spit out. It will allow you to see the parallel realities," he said.

"You want me to chew it now?" I asked.

"No. First we need music. Come with me, my amigo," he said.

"And this plant, from your garden, it can open doors in the brain?" I asked.

"Si. With music! This plant, it loves the music. The music, the melody, even the melody of the voice; not what is said, but the way magical words are said, they can open doors in the brain and to other realities," don Rojas replied.

We entered the hacienda through the double stained glass doors and were immediately greeted by the "Oriental" servants who said nothing, but made as if to rub against us, but did not. don Rojas patted them across the head, scratched their ears, and sent them on their way.

I told don Rojas about my hallucinations and experience with the Demon Princess Queen and her minions, some of which were cats.

don Rojas replied, "Si! I know her well. She is very beautiful. Powerful. You were wise to resist, or she would have taken your soul, and made you a slave."

"So, you're saying that was not a hallucination?" I asked.

"Si. A parallel reality," he answered.

"If it was real, then Sophia saved me," I added. "Or I wouldn't be here now," I admitted. "She even helped me find the way to the ranchero."

don Rojas gave me a serious, yet questioning, thoughtful look. Then laughing and slapping me on the back, said, "Ella debe gustarle! Sophia she grows a woman's heart! But beware, my gringo amigo, a woman's heart is like the bird, and may fly away."

don Rojas led me into the "music room;" the same room I'd seen that night Sophia sent me back to the Pemex gas station. It was de ja vu all over again, and as ornate and richly furnished as the rest of the hacienda, except that, it was crowded with musical instruments, horns, a clavichord, harps, drums, and a large assortment which don Rojas happily named: Lyres, bucinas, kinnors, crwths, ocarinas, lurs, ouds, citoles, mibiras, opharions, and an organistrums.

"These are for magic," he answered. "La música of the spheres. They will open for us windows and doors to the parallel realities."

don Rojas instructed me to break off and chew a chunk of the bulbous purple fruit from his magic garden. I was handed a silver, bejeweled cup, and he me instructed to sit on the floor, and to spit out the fruit into the cup when the taste became unbearable.

As I chewed don Rojas explained to me the nature of some alternate realities, and parallel dimensions, and the little holes he said acted as passageways between them.

"First, you must understand, what you think is magic, is realmente ciencia! Science. La tecnología del futuro es la magia de hoy," he said.

"Are you saying there is no magic?" I asked between chews. "That it's really an advanced form of scientific technology?" I asked. "From the future?"

"Si and no. Someone living 200 years ago, would think the television or the radio is mágico. Magia. Si?"

"Yes," I agreed.

"Si. Esta tecnología I explain to you now, is not from the future, but from the past," don Rojas explained. "This is secret knowledge. Conocimiento secreto. Sagrado. Sacred."

"This stuff tastes terrible," I said, still chewing.

don Rojas continued: "I told you about the alternate dimensions, and the holes in the barriers that separate these realities, Si? With sounds, music, special chemicals which release much energy, these holes may be made larger, so large, one can cross over; and demons may do so, to steal bodies and souls. A true sorcerer, a man of knowledge, can open these holes and command the demons to do as he wishes."

I spit the remnants of the plant into the silver cup. "Yes, I remember. I have it all down in my notes," I replied. "How many demons do you command?"

don Rojas laughed. "Demonios? Many hundreds, some quite beautiful, but be careful, they may bite off your head."

"I'll remember that. How many dimensions are there?" I asked.

"Only the gods know," he answered. "In some dimensions the demons dwell.

One must beware. Be Careful. That's the truth. In some parallel realities, you also dwell. A twin."

"What?" I said in surprise.

"Yes, a twin, but not a twin. Close but no cigarro!" he said with a laugh and then encouraged me to chew more of the magic purple plant from his garden. "Chew," he insisted.

I did as instructed. The taste was extremely bitter and foul, like a mixture of dead skunk and radioactivity.

don Rojas continued to explain: "You have hundreds of twins who live in dimensiones paralelas with different histories, politics, leaders; worlds which may be similar but unlike our own. Some twins live in realidades paralelas almost identical to our own. Others live in the futures, others in the past. Through the holes you can look at your twin, and gaze into the past, but you cannot cross over, except as a soul. Hacer lo contrario esto es impossible."

"Why is that?" I asked.

"Because the universe is in balance," he explained. "One can't add or take away, only change from matter to power, from power to matter. The same body cannot exist twice in the same dimension, in the same reality. Consciousness may split, become many, but only one of your body is all there can be in a single reality. And yet, all are connected between the dimensions, which allows the soul to travel between realities."

I spit the remnants of the purple plant into the silver cup. don Rojas insisted I chew what was left of the bulbous purple fruit.

"Today you will not visit your twins, but the twin realities, of which, how many, only the gods can know," he said. "But you will visit as a soul, in spirit-body. Your real body, empty of the soul, will stay here."

"Didn't you say that was dangerous?" I asked. "So far, all my experiences have been rather dangerous."

"Si. To visit other dimensions, as a soul, is dangerous," don Rojas explained. "Because, to leave the body behind, invites possession by demons and souls looking for a body."

"Yes, I remember," I replied between chews. "So why is this a good idea?"

"I will watch over you," he answered.

I stopped chewing, and spit out the last of the plant into the bejeweled silver container.

"How can you watch over me, my body, if I'm in a different reality?" I asked.

"You will not travel in the body," he answered. "You will travel like through the telescope, looking through the window, opening the door and looking inside at parallel realities which exist side by side. You will pass through the tiny holes in las membranas that separate the realities. But be careful. Avoid the dark side. Stay in the light. Do not let anyone touch you."

"Why not?" I asked.

"Because they may not let go," he answered.

"But you said I would be traveling as a spirit!

"Si. That is true. So be careful. No touch."

Fuckin' A. I had some damn serious doubts about this. But, one must not take counsel of their doubts, right? Right.

don Rojas positioned the silver cup so I was holding it with both hands, in my lap. Removing a jewell encrusted decanter from an enclosed glass case, he sprinkled some of the oily liquid into the silver cup. From within wafted a strong, but pleasant odor, fragrant like incense.

"Breath in. Breath out. Breath in," he said, and I did as instructed.

Retrieving a flute-like instrument, he put it to his lips, then stopped and said: "Remember: These holes can also lead to alternate realities and dimensions where dwell many dangerous diablos, aliens, and demonios. If the beautiful woman invites, say no. Do not let anyone touch you. Always choose the light, not the darkness. If you see a beautiful demonio, you run! Beware. That is the truth."

"Understood," I said.

don Rojas put the flute-like instrument to his mouth and began playing an eery, curiously weird melody, producing an almost physical hum that vibrated along the skin of my body. The jewels embedded in the silver cup began to flicker with light. Gradually, a ghostly-greenish tendril of smoke emerged from the silver vessel, writhing and curling like a snake, the head of which was completely black, pulsating, mushrooming outward, glowing, dilating, forming an aperture, a tunnel floating in mid-air in front of my face, but tied to a thin-curling-twisting-string of smoke that led back to the silver vessel.

don Rojas laid aside the flute. Picking up a horn-like instrument, he put it to his lips producing a sound something akin to a fog horn. The black-hole aperture was becoming larger, now exceeding the height of don Rojas; and then, like the head of a titanic snake, and with a curving dive, it struck, enveloped and swallowed me up, and the next thing I knew, I was in an electric blackness.... and emerged into a sparkling orange-red effervescence where there was nothing beneath my feet, as if I had stepped off the edge of a cliff. I could see miles below, convinced I was going to fall to my death...

I didn't fall down. I was was floating, drifting, in an all encompassing, multi-membraneous-multi-dimensional-soap-bubble-like-infinite-universe; and all around me, above, below, on either side: a jumbled and juxtaposed landscape of semi-transparent, distorted things intersecting, merging, passing through one another and occupying quadrants of space which defied any sense of gravity or direction or up or down... objects resembling vehicles, birds, houses, trees, flying vehicles, toasters, lamps, a ghost ship, bookcases, a lion leaping, a man-like entity upside down, space-ships, bizarre alien creatures, titanic insects, exploding planets, dinosaurs, flying reptiles, and men-like creatures dressed in flowing robes flying upside down through the air only to be intersected by a ghost ship, both passing through the other unharmed; babies born, old men dying, women raped, clouds on fire, oceans boiling, death, birth, war, endless wars... and the laughter, cries, screams, noise of engines, machines, animals, a confused cacophony of sound... and everything was constantly changing and in flux: flat, elongated, round, inside out...

Disembodied I am flowing, faster, sucked toward a cloudy-mirror-like membraneous-pool of a thin water-like-substance which is reflecting, mirroring me and which separates and hides this reality from a world parallel to our own. I struck the shimmering watery surface and slammed into the mirror-image-of-me-arriving from another direction, another reality. I emerged in a world, an America similar to but different from our own...

I'm a disembodied spirit standing in New York City's Time's Square. The year is 1969. I'm watching, listening to the giant electronic television-billboards which dominate the streets.

"War with Mars!" "Nuclear tipped missiles are on the way!" scream the headlines.

On some of the television billboards, "talking heads" blue-suited newscasters are discussing what is happening and why.

On one electronic billboard, a newscaster and a panel of experts are explaining the history: "It had been believed, since ancient times, that Mars was a living planet, its blue colors suggesting oceans, the changing white marbled surface believed to be clouds," explained one astrophysicist to the nodding head of the newscaster.

"And a magnetic field had been detected," explained a second astrophysicist, "almost ten years ago."

"Why would a magnetic field be important?" asked the newscaster's talking head.

"A magnetic field provides the Martian atmosphere and oceans, and any living creatures down below, with a magnetic shield and protection from powerful solar winds and radiation," the expert explained. "If Mars had lost that magnetic shield, its atmosphere and oceans would have boiled away and disappeared into space. Except for fungi and bacteria, life could not thrive under those conditions."

The talking head now asked his other guests, a Rabbi and a Bishop: "Isn't it true that until 1965, religious leaders and politicians insisted that life, except on Earth was contrary to God's will, and there was no life on Mars."

The Rabbi answered: "That was the opinion of the Catholic Church. We have always known that god created humans on Earth, in the image of god. If there is life on other planets, even if these Martians look like humans, they could not possibly be human."

"How do we know they are not human?" asked the newscaster's talking head.

"Because they couldn't possibly have a soul," replied the Rabbi.

"You don't know that," insisted the first astrophysicist.

"It is written," replied the Rabbi, "in the Bible, the Talmud. Man was created in the image of God, and became a living soul. If God had created man on Mars, God would have said so in the Bible."

"These creatures on Mars, are not human, but devils without souls," added the Bishop.

The camera swiveled over to pugnacious face of Vice President General Le-May: "That's why we will destroy them. Bomb them back to the stone age. They are barbarians. Subhumans. Our democracy, our American way of life, our entire planet is at risk. If not eradicated these godless Martian savages will eventually attack our planet."

"I disagree," the astrophysicist interjected. "In 1965, when the Mariner space craft beamed back the first hundred close-up pictures of Mars, we saw great cities, monuments, titanic temples, but no evidence of any technology comparable to our own; and no sign of war. Of course the Martians have souls. And they appear to be peaceful and highly intelligent."

"Intelligent? You mean sneaky! If they're so peaceful, then how do you explain what happened to Mariner 5? And the Russians Zond 2 spacecraft?" exclaimed the Vice President. "They were attacked and destroyed, as sure as God made green apples."

"You don't know that," argued the second astrophysicist. "More likely, those two spacecraft malfunctioned or crashed."

"That's where you're wrong again," General LeMay insisted. "We've known since World War II that flying saucers have our world under surveillance. We've released all this data in Project Blue Book, which proves, convincingly, without a doubt, that flying saucers have been visiting Earth. And, I can think of only one reason: They are from Mars and they are planning to attack."

"But isn't it true, Mr. Vice President, General LeMay, that 90% of UFO sightings have been dismissed by the military as lacking credibility?" The talking head newscaster asked.

"Yes, but the other 10% consists of definite proof," LeMay replied.

"And how do you know they're from Mars?" asked the second astrophysicist. "There's no hard evidence. Attacking Mars is so extreme, its irrational."

"Extremism in the defense of liberty is no vice," LaMay stated emphatically. "And we have the proof, a UFO which crashed in the deserts of Nevada in 1947, and which is still being examined in the 'Blue Room' in Hangar 18, at Wright-Patterson Air Force Base."

"No one, except the military, has seen this so called space craft," the second astrophysicist countered, "and even if what you say is true, we don't know it's from Mars,"

"The data from Mariner 6 and 7," argued the first astrophysicist, "confirmed that technologically, the Martian are at or near the level of the Roman and Egyptians empires thousands of years ago. They are highly cultured and sophisticated but they have no technology to speak of."

"What we are doing is wrong," argued the second astrophysicist. "We are about to turn Mars into a nuclear waste land. Think of all the knowledge we could have gained, all we could have learned, if we'd sent a peaceful mission to Mars, instead of having this irrational knee jerk reaction and rush to war. It's a catastrophic loss to science."

"No, its god's will," stated the Bishop.

"Amen," agreed the Rabbi.

"Well, its too late to argue about it now," said the smiling face of the Vice President. "Our eagles have landed!"

Transmitted on every television across the world, and as shown on every television-billboard on Time Square, hydrogen bombs were exploding across the face of Mars, as Americans celebrate and cheer.

....Disembodied, I am sucked toward another nearly-invisible membrane punctured by zillions of microscopic holes... and not just my disembodied spirit, but atoms, molecules, and gases are leaking across... and going in both directions! There is an exchange of energy, particles and mass between realities and dimensions through these infinite tiny holes...

... and I enter another separate reality, then another, each darker than the other... there are parallel realities where the Kennedy brothers were never killed, realities where Franklin Delano Roosevelt died from polio before he became president and Hitler and Japan won the war... realities where humans never evolved... realities where dinosaurs still dominate the earth... dog stars where eons ago a species of Canus Lupus evolved into human-like creatures after they took to the trees, developed grasping hands, climbed down, stood on two legs, developed language, technology, and where, now, protests rage demanding "save the cats" or "save the squirrels"...and parallel realities where aliens from far away worlds-- some looking distinctly human and others monstrous and depraved--have conquered other alien worlds; and not through atomic weapons, but diseases genetically engineered to kill or enslave....

... and somewhere, in my mind's eye, I wonder if this is real, or a hallucination-dream...

....Disembodied, I flow toward darkness and the passageway of a billion tiny holes... Souls, spirits, molecules, atoms, particles, energy, all are leaking from one parallel dimension to the other, passing through these membranes... and I am overwhelmed with understanding: this leakage, these holes, establish and maintain a homeostasis which prevents any dimension from expanding or collapsing beyond certain limits which would bring destruction to all...

...and I, a disembodied spirit, am sucked toward a nearly invisible membrane; again I see and then pass through an approaching double of me, a twin, a reflected image of myself, only to emerge into a darkening reality...I experience one parallel dimension after the other... sometimes lingering, sometimes quickly moving on to yet another, each of which becomes darker, dream-like...

...I emerged into another parallel reality that darkly shadows our own: My disembodied spirit stands upon an Earth of boiling oceans, flaming skies, cities in smoking ruins, everywhere dead bodies of animals and humans broiling in the heat... and ghoulish wraiths, shadowy goblins and succubi, creatures demonic and devilish, are feasting upon the corpses festering in the fires, blazing heat and smoky haze of the sun. Claws ripping away and drooling mouths biting into and consuming bloody arms, legs, eyes, bones, hearts, livers, brains, squirming flesh... and there are tendrils of ghostly souls being sucked from those dying and newly dead...

Although I am but disembodied spirit, many of the ghouls lift their snouts, sniffing the air, and some begin to slither, hobble, and crawl toward me, some are spider-like, with upside down heads and mouths where mouths were never meant to be; drooling, stuffing pieces of bloody flesh into gaping jaws as they ooze and stumble toward me... Fascinated, I feel no fear and wonder if this is a dream... closer they come, and others began to follow, creatures with spiders' legs, the heads of flies, the chests and arms of apes, bodies of goats, the faces of pigs with distended breasts of old women, closer, closer, from all directions, grunting, moaning, jabbering, oozing, drooling, leaving a trail of slime in their wake....

A young woman, blonde and beautiful, flowers in her hair, robed in sparkling silver and gold Grecian dress, emerges, like from a dream, and runs toward me, holding out her hands. Her face is kind, sweet, concerned. Is she afraid? Desperate to escape? In need of help? She is breathtakingly lovely!

The ghouls are coming closer. Taking my disembodied hand, she quickly leads me away into a cloud-like fog, into a dreamy castle-like hall from the walls of which protrude human arms and hands holding candles lighting the way. She stops, turns toward me, and radiates goodness, purity, nurturance, safety, beauty, love...and... a need to be protected...And I want to protect her!

She wraps her arms around me, kisses me passionately, and... Then... metamorphosis, her face has become a hideous, snarling, twisted, snapping, drooling, jaw-fanged devilishly reptilian insect... I arched my head away from her saw-blade teeth and try to escape her grasp... but her arms are locked around my body, fingers have become claws digging into my back, deeper, deeper, through skin, muscle, sinew... There is excruciating pain! This is no hallucinatory dream! And I realize, this hideous demonic creature is going to rip my heart and soul from my body... I can't escape.

Her jaws are snapping at my face, claws digging through my back tearing aside the muscles, tendons, shoving aside my spine, reaching inside me, my back arch-ing backwards, muscles ripping...The pain is horrendous. She's taking hold of my heart, her clawed-hands are about to burst from my chest... I'm losing conscious-ness...sure I am about to die... and now there are fingers tearing into my shoul-ders, pulling, dragging me...

I open my eyes. I am lying on the floor of the hacienda, in the music room, gazing up at the concerned and worried face of don Rojas.

9. Passageways to Separate Realities. Transmigration of Souls: To Die and Be Reborn

I lay upon the floor, my back in terrible pain, feeling angry, confused and afraid. Opening my eyes, I gazed up at the concerned face of don Rojas.

"I think you took the wrong turn at the Albuquerque," he said with a laugh. "You should have taken the right turn at the Kookamunga!"

I stood up. My back hurting, muscle cramping, legs unsteady. I'm in no mood for levity.

"What's that supposed to mean? God damn it! Some creature just about tore my heart out and you think its funny?" I said, angrily.

I lifted up the back of my shirt, sure there were claw marks and rips deep in my back. "Tell me? What's this look like to you?"

don Rojas gazed at me with concern: "Si. Bruises. Did I not warn you? No let anyone touch?"

"Yes, but..." I began to say in protest, trying to remember: did I touch her first or did she touch me first? Didn't matter. We touched.

don Rojas opened a satchel hanging from his neck, and removed some flowery substance.

"Chew this, then swallow. It will make the pain go away," he said.

I did as instructed.

"Did I not warn you?" don Rojas said again. "Stay away from the dark side."

"That's not fair," I replied. "I had no way to control where I was going."

"Did you look at the dark side?" He asked. "Did the darkness not make you curious?"

Fuckin A. He was right. I didn't obey his instructions.

don Rojas patted me affectionately on the shoulders: "My amigo. I was watching over you. When I saw you were in the danger, I stepped in and pulled you back to this reality. Your back will heal quickly. Only your pride has been injured."

"My pride?" I said angrily.

"You are angry because you were afraid. All men feel fear. Even sorcerers," he answered.

"Hey! It's not my ego that got hurt. I could feel her claws digging in my back."

"Has the pain gone away?" He asked.

"Yes."

"And what did you learn about the realidades paralelas?" he asked, changing the subject.

"Nothing that made sense," I admitted. "Except, maybe, the universe is a multi-dimensional soap bubble; but I don't buy that at all. I think it was just a drug-induced hallucination."

"You are wrong, my amigo," he answered. "What did you aprendido? Think."

"I learned what I already knew: This is not the only reality," I answered.

"And what else?" He asked.

"There are parallel realities which mirror and shadow our own, and some of them are hellish, nightmarish," I replied.

"And what else did you aprendido?" He asked.

"It seemed to me that each reality, these parallel dimensions are separated by a double membrane each membrane containing its own separate reality, and between them, there's an extra-dimensional space, a gravitational void."

"Is it a void, or passageway?" he asked.

"I don't know," I answered.

"Maybe what you found is the trans-dimensional hallway infinito in length, between all the membranas; a camino de separating all the realities and leading to all the other doors to all the other dimensiones paralelas within the infinity of the universes and its many mundos extraños."

"Maybe? Then you don't really know, do you? And if that's true, what's the point of having a passageway if you don't know where it goes?" I asked.

"The passageway, it can be a place to hide from enemies. It may be the pathway which leads to all other worlds. Want to go to the Mars? Maybe the next galaxy? Step into this pasillo infinito and find the door. This is how the creatures of the cosmos can journey to our world. Through these holes, into this passageway which lead not just to other dimensions and realidades paralelas, but alien worlds."

"Have you visited alien worlds?" I asked.

"Si. One can visit another reality, another world, and learn their technology, or take it, and bring it back to this world. These are the doors to knowledge. Power."

"Seems to me these doors only open to Hell." I answered.

"And this is why, my amigo, I keep so many doors in this hacienda locked. Magico can kill."

"You're saying, you have technology from other worlds locked in some of these rooms?" I asked.

don Rojas ignored my question and instead led me from the "music room," then downstairs back toward the palatial hall.

I wasn't happy. My back hurt. All these experiences had been nothing but bummers and bad trips. I also had the suspicion don Rojas was lying to me. Technology from other worlds that he keeps locked up in his hacienda? I had serious doubts about that. The mirror and skulls? Maybe hallucinogens in the incense and vapors. But if he was just lying and trying to manipulate me, or, if he was really telling the truth, then, why? What did he want from me? And all this wealth! How did that fit in? He couldn't have acquired all this by making rain or selling cures to the peasants!

So, I asked him: "If knowledge is power, then why are you telling me all this, and sharing your knowledge?"

"Perhaps, my amigo, maybe I shall make you my apprentice. Or maybe not," he said, and began laughing.

"Oh really? Why me?" I asked.

"Because a man who died and who is not supposed to exist, yet exists, and who was visited by the Trinidad, is a sign he has been chosen, has special purpose. I may learn from you the secrets, of the Trinidad," he answered.

I looked at him askance. I had not yet told him of my second encounter with those three entities.

"What I don't get" I said, "is why you've chosen to live like a king? I have trouble understanding why a sorcerer, a man who loves knowledge, would love so much luxury. Where did you get all the money? By conjuring it out of thin air? Stealing it from other planets? And all this," I said with a sweep of my hand, "How'd you get this stuff? I thought the Conquistadors destroyed everything and melted down the rest and shipped it to Spain. Or are these copies of originals?"

Hearing footsteps coming up behind me, I spun around. But it was no demon, just a little devil: Sophia had entered the great hall, walking in glorious beauty, like the twinkling stars of endless night. My angry mood stepped aside in favor of love and desire!

"Hello, Sophia," I said in greeting, giving her my most charming, dashing smile. "You look incredibly beautiful!"

Stepping up to her father, she kissed him on the cheek, but ignored me like an ill wind.

"What are you doing, papá?" she asked sweetly.

don Rojas answered: "This room, the artifacts. Our amigo is curious how I obtained my wealth, and where we acquired these priceless treasures."

"I thought all this stuff was destroyed and melted down by the Conquistadors," I added.

Sophia, her emerald green eyes flashing, hissed: "Montezuma was a fool. But his brothers were not and hid these treasures where they could not be found by greedy Spanish eyes." Sophia added: "Montezuma should have killed Cortez and his men as soon as they stepped to shore. That's what I would have done."

"But you were there, my daughter," don Rojas interjected. "It was prophesied, it was the will of the gods."

"Sophia, how'd you get there? Did you travel back in time?" I asked, masking my disbelief.

Sophia wrinkled her nose and frowned in reply: "You are a child. You understand nothing."

"Please, enlighten me," I replied.

"Six hundred year ago I was reborn Toani Moctezuma, a priestess; my mother Aztec royalty, a beautiful sorceress from Acatlan, her mother a sorceress from Tenochtitl. I inherited their gifts. Cortez thought me a witch, wanted to kill me, then forced me convert to Christianity and to marry a conquistador. I killed that Spaniard, my husband, with poison. Then, I am forced to marry again, and again the poison. And a third time, and he died too. They wanted to use me to make royal babies, royal sons to rule the people for the Spaniards. No. Never."

don Rojas gave Sophia an affectionate smile and said: "Thanks to my daughter, Sophia, who long ago lived, we found these treasures, which for 600 years had been hid."

Honestly, I found it all very hard to believe.

"There is much buried treasure in the world," he said. "There are long lost graves and caverns laden with incredible wealth; some hidden by the rich and powerful while they still lived," don Rojas explained. "Once they, or those who helped bury these treasures, die, and live again, they may remember where the wealth was hid."

"Are you saying you got this wealth, because of memories from your past lives?"

don Rojas smiled and merely shrugged. Sophia, for some mysterious reason, was obviously angry and glaring at me with daggers in her eyes; like she was sighting down a gun barrel pointed at my head.

What the hell was she pissed about? I'm the one who should be angry! Women, their moods--I don't understand women!

She said, "I have much to do, papá. I will tell you about the funeral at dinner." With a toss of her hair, and nose in the air, and giving me once last poisonous evil eye, she departed the hall like a queen.

"We shall have dinner soon," don Rojas said to me. "Let us have a short walk before the sun sets."

We headed for the front double door, first walking past many more rooms of fabulous wealth. I was frankly finding it impossible to reconcile all this luxury with my stereotype of a sorcerer's style of life. don Rojas' home certainly bore no resemblance to the Shaman's dwelling I encountered in the central highlands of Vietnam. Of course, I wouldn't want to live in a jungle hut either.

"I mean you no offense," I said, "But it seems to me incongruous that a seeker of knowledge would also be a seeker of so much luxury; even if you or you daughter did know where it was hidden in a past life."

don Rojas looked at me in the eye: "You are a warrior, a seeker of truth, Si? Yet, you are also a warrior who loves to fight, who takes pleasure in killing those who deserve to die, Si?"

"Well, yeah, but only in self-defense," I answered.

"Have you ever wondered why?" he asked.

"My upbringing, genetics, traits I inherited, all play a role, I'm sure," I said.

Don Rojas replied: "And your past lives, the silver thread, are also inherited and shapes your life today. What were you when you lived and died so long ago? Warrior! Priest! Scientist! Pirate! A killer of men! A child who loved the sea! All these lives, this soul lives on, and makes you what you are today. There is no escape. I too have lived past lives, and they too make me what I am today."

"For example?" I asked.

don Rojas replied: "Hace casi setecientos años, I was reborn a warrior priest, the eagle my spirit guide. I became king, un emperador, the emperor, Acamapichtli, the Tlatoani of Tenochtitlan, and would sacrifice to the gods for wisdom, power. Many daughters and sons, a dinastia I sired. Many beautiful bailarinas and esposas lay in my bed.   Acamapichtli had great love of power, riches, women, and beauty, and he surrounded himself with all. And why not?"

"Si. It's all illusions," don Rojas added, "but its my and his alma reborn; and in my blood, Está en mi sangre. So, like you, I have a desire for beautiful women, and I live like a sorcerer Emperor King."

Then don Rojas asked, half-mockingly: "Would it be better if I lived like a peasant in a hut made of mierda y ladrillo?"

Yes he certainly lived like a sorcerer king. But, this life-style, was not for me.

"Do not judge to harshly," don Rojas said, as if reading my mind. "This hacienda has many habitaciones secretas, laboratorios, dedicado to the study of the chemistry, the magnetism, the technologies, and the discovery of hidden treasures of knowledge and the riches of the mind. Behind many doors, I shall open for you some day, are inventions and discoveries from other worlds, other realities, and the ancient past, which are like magico. And this tecnología mágica must be studied, to be understood and be useful. Knowledge is power but power costs money and money creates power."

"There is a lot of poverty in Mexico," I replied. "Did you ever consider giving away your wealth? Donating, at least, some of it, to charity?"

"Si. A los hospitales. A los huérfanos. Universidades. This I do. But one must be cautious, not make others curious, not draw attention to the wealth."

The sun was setting. Almost all the workers were leaving or had left. But where were they going? Where'd they gone? There were no cars arriving or departing to take anyone home. I counted six outbuildings, a stable, chicken coop, pig sty, one huge barn, and a five car garage. There were no living quarters for laborers I could see. And yet, some of the workers were...

"Do your workers live here, on the ranch?" I asked.

"Many do. Some prefer trees, caves, the barn, under the porch, or holes in the ground," he answered.

"What the fuck? You have all this money and you make these people live in caves? Trees?" I asked, astonished.

don Rojas laughed and laughed, slapping his thigh. "Make? I command them to work for me, Si. In the evening hours they are free, and they come and go and live and sleep where they please."

"You treat them like animals!"

Again don Rojas laughed. "They are animals. Humans are animals, too. Si? My workers, the servants, are not human. They are familiars. I make them human. They are cared for, given good food, they are happy to be alive."

"Are you saying those are really animals, like chickens and pigs? And you changed them into humans? So they can do work for you?" I asked, incredulous.

"They are spirit helpers, my gringo amigo. Fantasmas. Espíritu. Almas. Souls of animals waiting to be reborn. I give them the illusions of life, and for this they are muy agradecido!" he answered pleasantly.

Back at the hacienda, I showered and lay down for a brief nap before dinner, thinking and pondering all that happened since first meeting Sophia, then don Rojas, and all he'd taught me. Admittedly, I wasn't sure what to believe and had serious doubts--for to accept otherwise, to embrace it as real, and not the product of drug-induced delusional hallucinations and the power of suggestion, was to invite madness.

I couldn't sleep. The bed, the room, all this wealth, and the possibility that don Rojas and Sophia might be a little crazy and were messing with my mind... I didn't feel comfortable and got up to write my notes.

Later, as I entered the dining room. Don Rojas was just sitting down to table, which, to my delight, was set for three. Sophia made her grand entrance moments later, and, she looked good enough to eat! What a delicious babe! Hot damn I liked this girl!

She totally ignored me, instead, giving don Rojas a daughterly kiss, then sitting at table like a queen too haughty and proud to give notice to this love-sick peasant. She only consented to acknowledge my existence with a slight nod of her beautiful head, when I'd complimented her charms!

From the kitchen emerged three of the oriental ladies, bearing trays laden with dishes of foods served a la carte at staggered intervals. Jicama salad with avocado, citrus wedges and cilantro with chile piquin dressing. Chicken and hominy soup, sinaloa style, with jalapeño chile, tomatillo, spices, and lettuce. Chayote squash, huitlacoche and marinated in epazote herb and roasted garlic sauce. Chunks of white fish served in lime juice mixed with diced tomato, jalapeño chile, onion, green olives, avocado, and cilantro. Corn tortillas with oaxaca cheese and fire-roasted poblano chile strips and epazote. And all this before desert!

"There is no way we can eat all this," I said. "I feel stuffed just looking at it."

don Rojas smiled and replied: "Do not worry, amigo. Nothing here goes to waste. The ranchero has many mouths to feed."

Try and as I might to engage Sophia in conversation, she was as cold and frigid as a Siberian winter! What the hell was her problem?

I got the answer to that question as she regaled her father with details about Owl Woman's funeral, the weeping and lamentations, all the witches in attendance; then turning to me, and in a voice as sweet as honey, said: "Your girlfriend was there!"

"Girlfriend? Who's that?" I asked, mystified.

"The girl you love! Dancing Star!" she answered, her emerald eyes flashing cold blue steel.

It was like staring into the barrel of a gun!

I laughed: "What are you talking about? There's nothing between her and me. Nada! Besides," I added with my most roguish, charming smile: "You're my only girlfriend."

Sophia merely lifted her nose and said: "Ha! In your dreams!"

"Yes," I replied, "My dream girl, Sophia."

"Hmmf!" she said, her face a frown. "Your dreams. My nightmares."

don Rojas sighed, cleared his throat, tapped his plate with a spoon, then said, "Enough."

As dinner progressed, Sophia continued to give me the arctic shoulder but was the sweetest of daughters to her padre; chatting gayly then somberly about the funeral, who was there, what was said, the prayers, chants, oaths, incantations, displays of magic, and with emphasis: the handsome hombres. "Oh, la la!" she said gayly with a kiss of her fingers and toss of her beautiful hair.

Yours truly just rolled his eyes.

Finally, as coffee was served, don Rojas mentioned to Sophia that I did not believe in past lives.

Why do you think that?" Sophia asked.

"Because, there are probably more people alive now, than over the entire history of the human race combined. Two thousand years ago, there may have been less than 300 million humans world wide. Even in the 19th century there were fewer than a billion. Given the four billion people alive on this planet today, then there are not enough past lives to go around," I explained. "And hardly anyone remembers a past life."

Sophia gave me a condescending smile: "You think souls can only be reborn from souls on Earth? Or souls of animals cannot become human? Estúpido gringo."

"The beautiful Señorita is quite right. I am completely ignorant about these matters," I said. "But pray tell: why is it most people have no memory of a past life?"

"I can explain," don Rojas said, then took a sip of coffee: "Many do not remember because they were not human but animals, birds, fish. So many animals before humans! The animals they go extinct. The great herds, flocks of birds, schools of fish, lions, bears, wolves, so many animals before humans, now they are few. These creatures, they too had souls; the life force of the cosmos. What then happens to their soul when they die and there are fewer animals because the humans kill so many? Supply and demand, my amigo. The soul of the animals lives on and is reborn and becomes human when more humans are born. Piénsalo: One million bison die, another one million humans join the raza humana, but animated with the soul of the animal reborn."

don Rojas continued to explain: "When the animal soul is reborn human, what is it they can remember from the previous lives?" don Rojas asked. "Eating grass? Swimming in the ocean? Flying in the sky? Si, they might dream of swimming, flying, killing and eating animals, but these are dreams they think. Not past lives. There is nothing of significance, aviso de importancia, for most humans to remember from their previous lives. So they remember nothing of when they lived and died."

"And most people lived boring lives," Sophia added airily. "Waking up in the morning, eating, working, eating, sleeping. So what is worth to remember when that soul is reborn?"

"Many children remember, but then forget, or told, 'stop telling lies,'" don Rojas added. "Ah, but those who have led exciting successful lives and who have died rich or horribly, they will be reborn and may remember."

don Rojas continued to explain. "This will surprise you, my amigo. When a rich man dies, he may be reborn and have a similar life to the lives he lived before. Emperors. Kings. Conquering warriors and generals. Scientists, great philosophers, merchants who become fabulously rich: they posses a powerful life force, and when they die and are later reborn, they struggle to reclaim and continue their past life, and become rich and powerful again. A rich merchant may be born poor but becomes rich again. A general who dies and is born in a poor family, becomes a general again."

"For women, too this is neta, Eso que ni que. Many countries, in the ancient past, have been ruled by women, queens, empresses, or the kings have been ruled by the women. These women, they too are reborn, and become powerful and wealthy or marry the rich and powerful. The souls of powerful women will be reborn, and even if born poor, they will struggle and strive to again become queens, presidents, rulers of countries and industries, or to marry and rule the men who are the rulers."

don Rojas continued: "The rich, powerful, when they die, they are the tall trees falling into the river of life. Their soul lives on as waves and ripples along the sea of life. Their powerful life force, their souls are reborn and they strive to become emperors, kings, generals, conquerers, presidents, and powerful all over again."

"So, are you saying," I asked, "that the 'self made man' who is born into poverty and becomes a rich and successful man might be possessed of a life force, a soul, that once belonged to a rich and powerful man?"

Si!" don Rojas answered. "They may also be reborn and live other lives as well, and be not so rich and famous."

"And what happens if a man is reborn a woman?" I asked.

"Tal vez se convierte en homosexual," he replied.

don Rojas slid his chair from the dinner table and suggested we take an after dinner stroll and continue our conversation. Sophia consented to join us, which pleased me greatly.

Once outside, strolling in the moonlight, I observed the same strange menagerie of animals I'd seen when walking alone with Sophia in what may have been an alternate reality two nights before. Could these really be spirit-helpers, humans during the day, but now animals at night? No, it seemed too fantastic to believe.

Two cats approached and rubbed against don Rojas' legs, mewing a "meow" identical to that uttered by the Oriental servant girls that afternoon! But, how many ways can a cat meow?

The seven dogs resembling German shepherds and wolves, ran up and the two cats made a hasty retreat. Most of these big guys were friendly, but two were giving me the evil eye, growling. Sophia and don Rojas patted them all on the heads, scratched their ears and sent them on their way.

Could these creatures be the same men that ran to my car this morning? No. I laughed at the ridiculousness of the very idea.

"What is so funny? Yankee gringo man," Sophia asked.

"Just thinking about how much I love you," I answered.

Even in the moonlight I could see her smile with pleasure.

"You are loco!" Sophia replied.

"That's right. Crazy about you."

"No. You love Dancing Star," Sophia said, her voice angry.

"Sophia," I said, facing her, "whatever I've done to make you mad, I'm sorry. Lo siento mucho! It's my fault. I was wrong. You were right. I was insensitive. Please forgive me."

"You love Dancing Star. Putas," Sophia replied with her nose in the air.

"Ay caramba!" don Rojas exclaimed. "Ambos están locos por los murciélagos loco! ¡Detén esto ahora! Te comportas como un niño."

"Lo siento papa," Sophia replied, chagrined.

"Ay caramba!" don Rojas exclaimed for the second time. "Amigo? Tell us about the past lives you experienced after drinking of the bone-dust of the skulls."

In reply I recounted those lives which I most vividly experienced as I fell back in time, concluding with the ape-men episode.

don Rojas stopped in his tracks, and asked me: "Conoces la Biblia? La historia de Génesis?"

"Genesis in the Bible? Sure," I answered. "I know that story. My grandmother read it to me many times when I was a kid."

don Rojas replied: "El Señor Dios, the Lord God, he make workers, take care of his animals and gardens. Si? The Sky People, they say they are gods and make monkeys into men, make workers. Si?"

"Yeah, I guess that's one way of looking at it," I replied.

"Do you know of the hombre de las cavernas? The cave men? Neanderthals?" he asked.

"Yeah. Read about them. Why?"

"Genesis capítulo one. Dios hace al hombre ya la mujer. God makes man and woman. Genesis capítulo two Lord Dios makes more humans, but they have a soul. They are different from the men and women in chapter one. What is the job of those with souls, made in the image of Lord Dios? To take care of the animals, and the gardens!"

"I know what you're getting at," I relied. "But, my past-life experience with the ape-men had nothing to do with souls or the Bible. The Sky People were not gods, but weird silver-haired aliens. Maybe some of the other past lives I experienced were real, but that last one, I think, may have been a hallucination or a very vivid dream."

"So you say, amigo," don Rojas replied.

We strolled along a brick path which led to the river. The three of us stood admiring the view as the moon illuminated the trees and cast its reflection on the flowing waters. The night was alive with the sounds of frogs, insects, birds. A lone wolf howled in the distance.

"Was that the end of your journey?" Rojas asked.

"No," I answered.

We walked back toward the hacienda as I detailed what happened after my past life experience with the ape men and sky people, and my encounter with the white-on-white-triad of entities who offered to open the door to all realities

"That last experience, was probably a dream, or a hallucination," I concluded. "But if it was real, then those three things were coming for me, grabbing at my arms, and were going to drag me into another dimension. It was not a fun experience. I seriously doubt I would have come back alive."

"There were three? Una trinidad? Always three, and no more, no less?" don Rojas asked.

"Yes. Three," I replied.

"And they say they are the alpha and omega and ask you to go through the door?" he asked, his voice serious.

"Yes," I answered.

"And when you were the little boy who died, you also saw the three? The trinidad? Si?" he asked.

"Yes and no." I replied. "They weren't the same three, far as I can remember. Why is three significant?"

don Rojas excitedly explained: "The doors to the gates of knowledge! Desde el pasado antiguo! Since the long ago, across all cultures, chamanes, hechiceros, magos, men of knowledge have sought the Trinidad, the three gods as one, tres dioses como uno, who may open the gates to paradise and bestow knowledge and cosmic wisdom to those they choose."

"Why is the number 'three' significant. Why not four? Five? Or just one?"

don Rojas answered: "Tri' meaning three, and 'inity' means infinity Trinity is the unity of the oneness with the cosmos, to achieve the unity with all the things. The Trinity is the three dimensions, become one, time, but existing outside of time, but encompassing, que abarca, all of the space and time and the universe as a single entity, uno, the god of all."

"Tell me again, all that they said, what you saw," don Rojas demanded.

Again, I explained the visions, the words heard in my head when I encountered the tree entities who spoke of Alpha and Omega.

"You are certain of what they said?" don Rojas asked growing increasingly agitated and excited.

"As best as I can remember."

don Rojas was excitedly pacing back and forth, mumbling to himself: "I have searched all my life for the keys. And now, he has found it!"

"Found what?" I demanded.

"Ay caramba! To encounter the Trinity, to find this door, is the Holy Grail of sorcery and knowledge. You have found the three keys to the door!" don Rojas exclaimed excitedly. "The door that opens all doors!"

"What are you talking about?" I demanded.

"Ay caramba! The Trinity! The Trinity! Una trinidad! Don't you understand? Can't you see? The Trinity, they opened the doorway to all realities, to infinite knowledge, to the gods, and, they invited you inside! Ay caramba!

10: To See as Gods! A Door Opened - A Door Closed

"Ay caramba! The Trinity! The Trinity! Una trinidad! Don't you understand? Can't you see? The Trinity, they opened the doorway to all realities, to infinite knowledge, to the gods, and, they invited you inside! Ay caramba! -don Rojas

As we entered the hacienda, don Rojas asked the old lady housekeeper to make us coffee to be served in his study. Like every room in the hacienda, this room was richly furnished, with paintings by old masters, book cases crammed with ancient books and scrolls, and statues from Egypt, Babylon, Greece and Rome.

Coffee served, we took our seats and don Rojas then asked for step by step details leading up to my out of this world experience with the "three gods of the Trinity." He wanted to know all I'd done before hand, foods I'd eaten that day, what I drank and how much, words I'd said, and the exact sequence, steps, manner and method I employed in preparing, eating, smoking, drinking and consuming the last of the three keys which led to the encounter with the Trinity and doors to infinity.

"In the morning," he said, he and I would go in search of the flowery-resiny-vines which propelled me to the ultimate in alternate realities. These vines, I learned, are quite rare, and of which don Rojas had never before ingested as an ingredient in a mind-bending soup in the sequence I described. It was upon these vines that don Rojas had sprinkled his magic Mayan skull-dust. What don Rojas wished was for the three of us to repeat the sequence and call upon the three gods and "pray they open the doors and invite us to journey to the other side."

I really wasn't sure I wanted to take a trip to the other side--for fear there may be no coming back. The Demon Princess Queen and the blonde beauty tried to steal my soul... why should I trust three entities from another dimension just because don Rojas thought them gods and not devils?

There was a lot to be afraid of. What about those visions of me lying dead in the driveway of the hacienda, with bullets in my chest and brain? Was Snake Eyes on my trail? Would I be killed by his hands?

And then there were Owl Woman's frightful warnings and demands that I "go back" and "destroy evil." After much thought, I was now convinced that Terranza's son, and the priest who'd offered a bounty for don Rojas' head, were one and the same, even if he wasn't "black." The priest, I was sure, posed a real threat and danger, maybe to us all.

I had a very bad feeling. Maybe it was because of the Triad, or maybe it was because of that priest, or both!

Sophia laughed when I told them of my growing concerns.

"He offered to pay you a thousand Yankee dollars?" Sophia asked. "Only a thousand? Are we really worth so little? Did you hear this, Papa?" she said turning to don Rojas.

don Rojas looked at me and said: "This is why we have nothing to fear from that diablo worshipping padre. He is weak, has little power, which is why he must offer money to others to buy our souls and our deaths."

"We should have killed him, Papa. He is evil incarnate," Sophia replied.

I was thinking the same thing. That bad feeling was growing stronger.

"How do you know he's not planning to harm you?" I asked. "Maybe he's paying others, recruiting an army of witches, and is planning to lead them here. Owl woman said he's dangerous. I'm sure he's the one she said I should go back and kill."

don Rojas turned to Sophia and said, "Hija, ¿qué ves?"

Sophia closed her eyes, her brow furrowing in deep concentration. "I see nothing of this priest," she said quietly, her eyes still closed.

"And this is why," don Rojas said, as he slid his chair from the table, "Terranza's son is no danger to us. He is but one man, and has little power, compared to our own. And why should he seek vengeance now? Terranza died many years ago."

don Rojas stood up and said: "We have much to do in the morning. We must rest. Sleep. Dream. Buenas noches."

"Buenas noches, Papa," Sophia said in reply.

'Sophia," said I, "the evening's still young. Let's go for an after dinner moonlight stroll."

"Why?" she asked.

"To stretch our legs. It's good exercise. And, because I like you, a lot," I answered. "I love being with you."

"No. You love Dancing Star," she replied cooly.

"Goddam it, girl, why do you keep saying that? I, love, you!'

"Why?" she asked.

"Because you're smart, beautiful, fascinating, special, unique. A rare flower, and what's rare is for the rare," I answered.

"No. You think Dancing Star is more beautiful," Sophia answered.

I wasn't going to argue with this female nonsense, so instead I laughed and said, "Sophia, if you think she's so beautiful, then maybe you should go out with her."

"She's your girlfriend, not mine," Sophia answered cooly.

"Why did you send me back in time?" I demanded, changing the subject.

"Did I?" She innocently replied.

"Yeah. Twice. Why?" I demanded.

"Because maybe I did not like the choices you would make," she answered.

"Sophia! I'm here because I chose you. Not Dancing Star. You! But you are very dangerous! Loving then rejecting. Sending me back to that Pemex station! You are very difficult to deal with."

"Am I?" She innocently asked.

"Yeah. You steal a man's heart. Then step on it with your high heels."

"Did I steal your heart?" She asked.

"Yes!"

"I'm sorry. I didn't mean to. If I find it, I'll give it back to you in the morning."

What a bitch! But I kept that thought to myself. Instead, I laughed. Then to my disappointment she rose from her chair and said: "Buenas noches."

I took a long walk, by myself, in the moonlight--observed by myriad watchful eyes--thinking, worrying, and reconnoitering the surroundings, looking for any evidence of the priest, the Lt, or anything out of the ordinary. Of course, how could I possibly know what was or wasn't ordinary around here? I was being followed and watched by mice, goats, wolves, and who knows what other creatures of the night, and that sure didn't seem ordinary.

Finally, I made the trek back to the hacienda, then upstairs to the bedroom specially prepared for yours truly. Time to write my notes.

I sat at a hand carved, roll top, rococo style writing desk, putting thought to pen, recounting all that transpired since I'd last updated the log book which was now for my eyes alone. The $25,000 was tempting, but fuck it. The Company would never find out don Rojas even exists.

I was not comfortable sitting in that bedroom which was too luxurious for my simple tastes. Hand carved flame mahogany antique furniture decorated in gold leaf, a gold and silver crystal chandelier dominating the ceiling, thick Persian rugs embroidered in golden arabesques and complex geometric designs, paintings by the old masters, a baroque-style golden four poster kingsized bed decorated with rich carvings of magical beasts and floral motifs in silver and gold, and a private bath and toilet that may have been made of gold!

This place was like a museum. One false move and some priceless artifact would topple over and break! Then what? I'd have to pay for it? You break it you bought it? Everything was too fragile and too expensive. I would have been happier sleeping in the woods. Clearly I'd never been an emperor or fabulously wealthy in any past life.

What really piqued my interest, was don Rojas' mention of the many rooms in this hacienda which harbored secret alien technologies. If what he said was true, then it was this technological magic that I really wanted to get my hands on.

It was growing late. The next morning would be the start of a busy, exciting day.

Lights off, I lay wide awake. I'd always had a problem sleeping in strange beds; and this bed felt like it was made of sacks of money.

The solid mahogany hand-carved bedroom door slowly opened. Startled, I sat up. A shadowy figure crept into the room.

The Colt 45 was next to my pillow. Now it was in my hand.

Fuckin A! It was Sophia.

She stood before the bed, unbelting her little silk flowery thigh-high robe. It fell to the floor. Lacy black bra, heart-shaped red panties, garters, nylon stockings, blood red high heel shoes!

Fuckin A!

Lifting the covers she gazed down at my cock which was saluting stiff at attention. I always sleep in the buff, except when camping outdoors. Her gaze slowly, teasingly drifted from cock, to chest, to lips, to eyes... She gave me an innocent smile, then slipped next to me, took my cock in hand and then gazed into my eyes.

I wanted her! But no way was I going to fuck this heart-breaking beautiful sexy witch. All day she'd been a nasty bitch. She was playing mind games for sure. Stick my dick in her and I'd end up back at the Pemex station and would have to start this journey all over again.

Stroking my cock, she leaned close to kiss me. I pulled away and turned my head. Resist, resist, I told myself. Or its back to the cantina and the fat woman and her brats!

"Don't you love me anymore?" she pouted.

Taking a deep breath and then exhaling I replied: 'I love you very much Sophia. Just don't trust you. I know what you're going to do."

"Do you?" she asked. Sitting on her haunches, giving me an innocent look, she slipped her hands behind her back and unlatched her lacy bra.

Oh wow! She had such perfect upturned breasts, her nipples inviting my lips, fingers, hands which like my cock, began to respond as if they had a mind of their own.

Cupping her breasts she leaned close and offered them to my lips.

Oh Lord! My throbbing cock must have grown another two inches, but instead I resisted and turned my head away. It was a trick. She had been pissed at me all day. I was not going back to that fucking cantina.

"You don't love me," she pouted.

"Sophia! You're the woman of my dreams. I feel I've waited my entire life for you. I think your body is perfect. Perfect!" I said with emphasis. "But I don't trust you! You're going to transport me back in time, to that Pemex station and laugh about it. I know you! I know what you're up to!"

Sophia slid from the bed, stood gazing down at me and said: "You don't love me. You love only putas. You love Dancing Star."

"No babe. Only you!" I replied, my hungry eyes on her panties, garters, breasts.

Slowly she pulled her heart-shaped panties down to her thighs. My hard throbbing cock grew another inch, eyes locked on her neatly trimmed little bush. I wanted to do something to her body I normally am loath to do: She looked good enough to eat!

She unlatched one garter, then the other.

"Do you love me now?" she purred.

"Oh My God! Yes, but..."

Lifting a leg, her foot on the bed, she rolled down one nylon stocking, then the other, and then, slowly pulled her panties down, letting them drop to the floor.

Fuckin A!

"I promise you can trust me," she said in a shy, innocent voice.

Naked, she slid into the bed, took my cock, stroked it with her hand, and bent close, her lips within kissing distance from the throbbing head. She opened her little mouth to slip it between her sweet lips, but stropped, looked up at me with innocent eyes and said. "If you truly love me," she purred, "if you love only me... I promise..."

"Oh! Baby! Yeah! I love you! Only you sweet heart. Yeah. YEAH. LOVE YOU!"

I didn't get any sleep until dawn's early light, when I was awakened by a weight pressing against my stomach and rib cage.

Opening my tired eyes I gazed at a black crow standing on my chest. It cocked its head to the left and right staring at me as I stared back.

I looked around. I was back at the Pemex gas station.

"Oh fuck me!"

"What's the matter, baby?" Sophia asked.

I opened my eyes. We were in a richly furnished bedroom, in the same bed in which we spent a night of incredible heavenly sex. Sophia, gloriously, beautifully naked, was sitting, straddling my stomach, leaning upon my chest, her breasts, nipples, begging for my lips and eager touch.

"Nothing's wrong baby," I replied, "Everything is perfect!"

Taking her in my arms and rolling her over, we spent another glorious hour making true love...

... until the old lady housekeeper knocked on the bedroom door. "Breakfast will be served in thirty minutes. The master awaits you," she called, in Spanish, through the thick mahogany door.

Thirty minutes later I bounded down the spiral staircase, happy, in love, and eager to open more doors to another kind of paradise! The Trinity and the doors to all realities lay before me!

After breakfast, don Rojas and I spent much of that gloriously sunny day collecting medicinal and magic plants whose properties he explained. That evening, we would attempt to unlock the doors to infinite knowledge and take a journey to the realm of the gods.

I was wondrously happy, having found true love, and an invitation to become don Rojas apprentice. Sophia and I would be together for a long time, and, all that magic technology was waiting for me! don Rojas would teach me everything. I knew it! Everything was going great! And yet, I had this sense of foreboding.

"How do you know that its safe to call upon those three entities?" I asked. "I still have a bad feeling about this."

"We must be brave. Have courage," don Rojas answered. "One must risk all, to achieve all."

"I thought the trinity, in the Christian religion, is the sign of the cross: the father, son, holy ghost? Isn't that correct?" I asked.

"No," don Rojas replied. "The Christians make the three, into four: Father, son, holy, ghost, to fit the cross, which is the four seasons and the four corners of the world and cosmos. East, West, North. South. The Christians understand nothing of the true meaning of the Trinidad, which was known among the Aztecs, Mayas, Toltecs, Babylonians, and among the gods who first ruled ancient Egypt, 30,000 years ago; which is why I think you were chosen, invited to enter the doorway to all realities."

"What? Why is that?" I asked.

"Your past life with the ape-men and Sky People," he answered. "Dios. The lord god creates workers."

"Sorry. I still don't see the connection," I replied. "This also raises another issue, which is: how do we know the Trinity will show up and invite me again, and let you and Sophia come with me?"

"This we do not know," he answered.

"And, even more important: How do we know they'll let me come back?" I asked.

"This we do not know," he answered.

"Fuckin A. This sound like a very bad idea."

"You are wrong, my gringo amigo. Have courage. Do not doubt."

And yet, I had doubts. So far, most of my experiences with parallel dimension and separate realities, had ended badly. Twice now, nasty demons tried to steal my soul--unless it was all a hallucination. And the Trinity, despite their promises, did not seem all that friendly--they weren't just inviting me, they were coming for me! It would be just my bad luck, after winning Sophia's heart, to then lose everything, and get lost in some other reality with bullets in my brain.

Then, I remembered: Do not take counsel of your doubts. America is home of the brave, not the afraid. Of course, I wasn't in America, but Mexico!

Following a morning of gathering herbs and plants which don Rojas later prepared, Sophia and I spent the late afternoon making love. Two hours later, I'd completely forgotten my fears, and was becoming increasingly excited about the opening of the doors to all realities. In the interim and meanwhile, I worked on my field notes.

Later, that evening, Sophia, don Rojas, and I gathered outside, within a large enclosed brick patio. don Rojas had given explicit instructions, which he demanded we obey.

Gazing at Sophia like a hungry lion savoring steak, I desperately wanted to drag her back to the bedroom, ravish her delicious body and enter that paradise between her legs.

It wasn't just sex. I was crazy in love with her! And I was sure she felt the same! She was such a babe! Total Foxy Lady!

Sophia gave me a smile and blew me a kiss. I sent one back to her; at which point don Rojas sternly intervened.

"Debes controlarte a ti mismo! Prepare yourselves. Show the proper respect to the gods. If you can think only of sex, then go outside and relaciones sexuales like dogs. Follar como perros! Go! Go! Fuck like the dogs. Only then come back when you can think with your brain. Focus. Do not insult the gods!"

Sophia looked abashed and ashamed: "Lo siento padre."

"You, my gringo amigo. Necesitas ir a masturbarte?"

"Masturbate? No. I'm fine. Sorry."

"You are sure?" don Rojas demanded. "You can control the lust?"

"Yes. Sorry," I answered.

Sitting in a semi-circle, Sophia on one end, don Rojas between us, we followed the same sequence which led to my falling back in time and my encounter with the Trinity. We passed the pipe and smoked; waited twenty minutes and chewed the next substance on the list, washing it down with a Coca-Cola chaser. Put some of the same substance in a pipe and struggled to keep it lit. Then, 25 minutes later, drank a soup of the skull dusted resiny flowery-vines which tasted like dead skunk! WHAM!

Exactly as before, it was if I'd been blown into the sky and slammed to the ground by an exploding bomb. Mind spinning, stomach churning, my surroundings telescoped then microscoped, bigger and smaller, and smaller still...Before me: tiny black pulsating orbs floating in mid-air, expanding then shrinking and expanding in size and then becoming concave black ghostly "holes" floating in air, and which seemed to radiate a visual energy. My skin tingled with wave after wave of electric pulses.

I tried to turn my head, to look at don Rojas and Sophia, but could only catch a glimpse from the corner of my eye. Like me, they were unmoving, as if set in concrete.

Powerful cascading electric-like waves were washing over my body, increasing in intensity as the black holes coalesced, merged and grew greatly in size. No longer black, this titanic concave hole was now radiating a powerful, almost blindingly bright, impossibly pure white light which enveloped all. Colors and objects had become various shades of white distinguished by varying shades of gray, all superimposed, juxtaposed and embedded within the pure radiating light. Perspective was abolished. I couldn't hear any sound.

An entity, tall, humanesque, shining bright, yet indistinct, appeared within the incredibly bright white light and strode forward, majestic, god-like, growing larger, titanic, all encompassing, as if I was an insect, a microbe in comparison. And then, it seemed to encompass me, and then, it passed through as if it were but a cloud...

... and again I fell back in time... experiencing past lives... one hundred years ago, five hundred years, a thousand, ten thousand years ago, across the page of past lives...

Finally I am among the Sky People... I'm older, well muscled, bearded, platinum blonde...and tall, but not as tall as the Sky People who are rail thin, beardless and with hair of shining silver.

Although many of my kind live in the gated and guarded, miles-in-size Sky People compound of farms, fields, fruiting trees, animals and sky palaces, I reside near the tributaries of four rivers along with my wives, many sons, daughters and followers. We were the first to be allowed to depart the Sky God compound. There were too many of us to be kept within. Free to do as we please, required only to offer sacrifices of meat to the Sky People, we have created a village, with running water, sewage, and have fashioned complex tools with which to fish, hunt, cook, create elaborate garments, and weapons to slaughter and kill.

To my sorrow, we have killed many Ape-men and Ape-women. They have come among us, like savage brutes and violent animals, to rape, murder, and plunder what their minds are to dumb to create or understand.

A Sky God, a breaker of cosmic laws, has sought me out, because, he claims, I am his first born son, and the most dear to his heart. I stand before him, outside the Sky People compound, accompanied by my wolves.

Although I can hear thoughts, I am speaking with this Sky God using spoken words, because, strangely, the Sky Gods cannot hear me think. This Sky God calls himself "The Creator" and "The Father," claiming to have sired me, my brothers, sisters, wives and the others like us, because, he said, we had all been fashioned by his hand; a mixing of tissues part-god part ape-man, inserted into the wombs of the Ape-women, is what I understand.

This Sky God had violated the Cosmic Law.

"There's trouble in paradise," he explains as I listen to his thoughts. "There's been a violations of cosmic laws which govern our the Sky God's, right to have settled and colonized this planet... "

I learn there has been a rebellion, factions against factions among these people who call themselves gods. The Lord of these Sky People, here on Gai, following orders from the gods of the gods, demands our destruction before they depart the planet. Yet our Creator and his followers, whose crest is an apple and a snake, resists.

I probe and understand his mind and thoughts: my birth, my creation, and those of my brothers, sisters, and dozens of others like us, were not lawful, not sanctioned, and was forbidden by the gods of these gods. Nor was it according to Cosmic Law to create the hybrid two-legged animal-half-humans, which had been fashioned for the amusement of the People of the Sky...and the greatest crime of all, the Sky People, the men and women calling themselves "gods," had sex with their creations; sex with my daughters and those of my brothers, sisters, others of our clan. Daughters of man, had given birth to creatures resembling the Sky Gods, for the sons of the gods had sex with the daughters of our clan.

This Sky God is warning me that I, my wives, children, must hide and make our escape. The gods of the Sky gods had declared that Sky People must leave this planet, and destroy all the lives, all the creatures they had unlawfully created. The Sky Gods, and their Lord, have been ordered to hunt us down and kill us all.

"You are nephilim, Nephilim" he says to me, which means forbidden. "But in my eyes, you are my first born son."

Then the memory of this past life began to fade... and all became an encompassing oneness of blinding white light.

The triad, the three entities slowly took shape and form and became manifest in the swirling all encompassing pure whiteness; each entity radiating an aura of tremendous energy. As before, two were standing face to face, in profile. The third, was looking down but facing my direction; and, as before, they appeared to be conversing.

The humanesque entity in the middle, seemed to look up, then slowly raised an arm-like appendage and pointed directly at me. The two entities on its either side, turned their head-like visages. All were pointing. The Trinity took a step toward me, then another.

A voice boomed inside my head: "I am Alpha and Omega, the beginning and the end. He that dares to enter the doors to all realities shall gain infinite wisdom and shall never die."

"Come," they said, inside my head. "Eat of the fruit of knowledge and never hunger or thirst again. Drink of the sea of knowledge and live eternal life in this and all other worlds.

The three humaneque entities took another step, their arms up above their heads, touching, forming a double arched rainbow gateway shimmering within the sea of pure white light.

"Come with us and live forever," they said inside my head, "and become one with cosmic wisdom and the god which is one, the unity of all."

I tried to stand up, but instead, seemed to flow like a river in this sea of energy.

"Enter ye in into the doorways of heaven, for wide is the gate, and broad is the way, if though wishes to be a man of knowledge. For all knowledge, alpha and omega, the beginning and the end, to see all things in the future and the past, in all other worlds, and all realities, the infinite cosmos with the eye of god... all within your grasp."

"Come. Enter. See with the eyes of gods."

The double arched rainbow doors opened, revealing darkness and swirling spiraling pearls of light which telescoped into galaxies, stars, planets... as if I were hovering millions of miles above with the all seeing eyes of a god!

I seem to be floating in space... I see stars, planets, moons... My eyes telescoped... The blue and white marbled Earth is before me.

My mind... my mind... is expanding...I have understanding: Earth is a living god and has consciousness, a swirling mind of energy at its core, the Sun is a greater god which is conscious, the galaxy an even greater god... even the gods have gods who have gods... and all have consciousness... to be a god is to be conscious... to be conscious is to create...

I hear a voice, the three as one, speaking, inside my head: "Only those with eyes may see. Let those with ears, hear. Time is a circle, and those who seek to be first, will be last, and those who are last will be first only to be crushed by the wheels of time."

I have acquired billions of telescopic and microscopic eyes and can see all of Earthly life, but, in, reverse... everyone, everything moving, walking, swimming, flying backwards, faster and faster becoming a blur of backwards motion... adults becoming infants, then unborn... and the dead, rising from their graves, becoming younger, then infants, and they too are unborn... and the backwards cycles of death becoming life becoming infants then unborn, the backwards-in-time cycles of dearth, life, birth, unborn... repeating faster, and faster generation after generation, further, deeper into the past...

....and wars, un-death, un-destruction, dead soldiers rise, bullets and shell fragment erupt from their shattered bloody bodies which instantly heal and the soldiers attack and march in reverse... fallen civilizations rise in reverse only to become cities, towns, villages, tribes... progress in reverse.... then humans, trees, plants, birds, dogs, everything began evolving backwards, humans becoming hairy apes, apes undergoing metamorphosis becoming monkeys, then four legged tree-climbing and tunnel digging mammals... evolving in reverse... flowers became reeds and blades of grass... buried bones became flesh and then living dinosaurs, reptilian mammals, reptiles, amphibians becoming four legged then boneless fish in the sea...faster, spinning faster... Earth evolving in reverse, freezing, broiling, fungi ruling a desolate volcanic-fire belching world bombarded by meteors creating and uncreating a cratered molten planet in flame...

My vision draws back... I pulled further away...above it all... The spinning Earth shrinking in size, becoming one planet among many, then a solar system ringed with moons and planets orbiting a flaming sun... .

....and I saw another solar system and my eyes telescoped... and I could see a purpled-cloud-marbled planet... and my eyes telescoped and I could see the human-like inhabitants engaged in mutual self-annihilation; hacking, killing, raping, slaughtering, bombs exploding, poisonous gases drifting, cities toppled in ruins, their world enveloped in an all consuming planet-wide war...

My eyes telescoped... beyond that solar system to another world smothered in angry crimson clouds of debris and becoming a smoking cratered boiling sea of molten destruction as ocean of asteroids and meteors strike the planet, evaporating the seas, obliterating the great cities, and destroying all life...

My eyes telescoped...

...and I could see a star, a sun ringed with silver sailing ships, satellites trailing red-glowing sails miles in length and width, reflecting, capturing rays of the sun... and inter-planetary war... a war between solar systems... with titanic alien space ships raining destruction on a blue-marbled world and battling for supremacy and enslavement of the defeated...

And I hear the Voice: "Those with eyes, let them see and gain cosmic wisdom, and eternal life, for the knowing soul shall never die but will live again on many worlds and become one with the all knowing all."

....It's as if I am viewing from a trillion miles above it all. Thousands of solar systems became but single points of light in a spiral of stars and dust becoming the arms of a galaxy falling further away... and, from my god-like increasingly distant all encompassing view, these galaxies are joined by dozens of spiral galaxies... then hundreds of galaxies, a billion galaxies, trillions of galaxies, all growing smaller, more compact, from my increasingly far-away above-it-all god's-eye view...

....trillions of galaxies, now pearls of light, flowing in the same direction, smaller, becoming a sea of molecules and atoms in a circular whirlpool of motion as if draining into an invisible, titanic sucking black hole... an entire universe collapsing, imploding, disappearing into this draining whirlpool of nothingness... and then: eruption, the flow of atoms bursting out from the other end... in the opposite direction...becoming clouds of particles, then atoms, molecules, pearls of light... moons, planets, stars, galaxies growing all manner of life...

And I hear the Voice: "Behold the engines of creation, that which dies shall be reborn, creating the cosmic energies, the life force of which is all."

...and it was as if I was trillions upon trillions upon trillions of miles above it all... and I could see that there was more than one universe... hundreds, then thousands, then millions, then billions of universes...an infinity of universes, parallel universes, shadow universes, a cosmic soap bubble of infinite universes each consisting of trillions of spiral galaxies each with billions of stars and trillions of planets orbiting within spiraling galactic arms... an infinity of universes and parallel universes, shadow universes, universes in multiple dimensions, separate realities, each expanding then contracting, but out of phase from one another, like the cycling of an infinite sea of pumping pistons... collapsing, imploding, disappearing down the whirlpool hole of nothingness... then explosion, expansion, becoming atoms, molecules, moons, planets, stars galaxies... then contracting becoming a whirlpool--sucked down into the blackest of holes... and then the process repeats: the eruption of an infinity of universes collapsing and expanding and creating life... followed by a whirlpool of collapsing destruction...creation, destruction, creation, destruction, an endless cycle of an infinity of collapsing and expanding universes...like the pistons of a god-like cosmic machine, generating the energy, the life force that sustains the cosmos, the foundations of consciousness and the totality of god...

The Voice speaks: "The cosmos is infinite and self-creating. God is infinite and self-creating. All shall be reborn from darkness into the infinite light of cosmic wisdom, and those who harken to the voice of the gods, will be rewarded with the eternal resurrection of life and knowledge possessed by all the gods and enter the gateway that leads to all worlds, the cycles of creation and destruction, and then behold All."

My mind... my mind... I am understanding... Everything!

don Rojas, Sophia... I feel their presence. Where are they? I try to look at my hands, my arms, and I am not solid, but a spiraling stream of energy snaking backwards deep into a narrowing tunnel of swirling light at the end of which sits me...

...And I rise up, further away, above it all, achieving a god's eye view of the totality of all... an infinite sea of cyclic collapsing expanding universes becoming further away, smaller, molecular, until, viewed as a collective they collectively take form, have substance, an illusory solidity consisting of an infinity of molecular universes joining together to fashion a single universe, a single reality, a living all encompassing reality...

And I hear the Voice: "That which is born of the gods, becomes Spirit and lives eternal life in not just this world, but all worlds which are infinite and without number and becomes one which is God."

I feel intense pleasure, happiness... and a veil falls away... and I see... fifty Gods forming a circle ruling over all... and beyond them, a hundred lesser gods, and beyond them, a thousand lesser gods, and beyond them, hundreds of thousands of lesser gods, thousands of millions, millions of trillions, trillions of quadrillions of lesser gods... and they are... particles, atoms, molecules of life...and they form moons, planets, suns, galaxies...the foundations of consciousness....

Words pregnant with meaning, flow like a cool, refreshing rushing river through my brain: The universe in its totality is consciousness and is god, from which all emerges and all returns... all are a manifestation of The God of all realities of all dimensions of the infinite universes--a unity, a continuum of consciousness consisting of particles, atoms, molecules, moons, planets, stars, galaxies, universes, life...collectively, all comprise God from which emerges the genetic seeds of life containing all the genetic instructions for the evolution and metamorphosis of all life... in every galaxy, in every universe, in all realities....the genetics seeds are the templates of life throughout the cosmos... creating a continuum of cosmic consciousness which is the ultimate god, from which all emerges and all returns...

All things are a manifestation of god... particles, atoms, molecules, bacteria, plants, trees, fish, birds... humans... gods... All emerge from God, all return to God and become one with God which is all, the quantum continuum. All the universes in totality are but molecules and atoms comprising the all encompassing consciousness, the unity of One which is God...

God is all, every particle, atom, molecule, moon, planet, galaxy, universe, are but molecules in the mind of god and given form and existence by the consciousness of god, which is self-creating; a consciousness of consciousness which is God.

And I hear the Voice: "Blessed are the pure in heart with eyes that see: for they shall see God, become God, and achieve infinite cosmic wisdom, a unity with the oneness that is all."

And I am rising further up, my vision seeing all, and the infinity of gods coalesce and become Three which stand before a door to to all realities, to cosmic wisdom, infinite knowledge, to become one with God! To become God!

I feel nirvana-like pleasure, happiness... I am surrounded by the light of consciousness, the gates of paradise have opened... I stand before the paradise of Eden and the fruit of all knowledge... of all knowing... of cosmic consciousness My mind is expanding... I am understanding...

And I hear the Voice: "Enter these doors and gain infinite cosmic wisdom, live forever, and become one with God which is All."

The trinity have become One.

The door is open. I am almost inside... about to achieve infinite knowledge and touch the face of God!

Gun shots!

The One becomes three, and the Trinity of entities swirl and face the spiraling tunnel of radiating light within which snakes a thin twisting tubular silver thread linking my ghost-like-elongated-consciousness-extending-from-god-like-all seeing-infinity all the way back to my body at the end of the tunnel, alongside which sit Sophia and don Rojas. I feel their presence. They are beside me, here, but also there, at the end of the radiating swirling tunnel of impossibly pure white light.

The echo of more gun shots...

The Three entities flow like a rushing river, curling though the swirling tunnel of pure white light, back to the source...to Earth, to the door which opens to the hacienda where I, my body sits! I realize, with a shock the Trinity are leaving me at the far end of the tunnel that leads to all realities... and the door to my world, my reality, is becoming a shrinking aperture which is closing behind them!

I contract, rushing back, telescoping, microscoping... the solidity of All becomes molecular, atomic, pearls of light, an infinity of galaxies growing larger in an explosive expansive creation...I am flowing closer and I see a trillion galaxies... closer and see a million galaxies... then a thousand galaxies.... I am growing smaller, coming closer, rushing flowing following the sliver thread, my soul, which leads back to a single galaxy, a beard of stars, our sun, solar system, Earth...

The tunnel is narrowing, contacting... I feel the presence of don Rojas, Sophia, we are three silver threads rushing back to the source, to our bodies... The door is closing, closing, our souls are not going to make it back to our bodies...I will be lost forever on the other side of reality.

An explosion of gun shots!

The door closes. I am high in the air, looking down on my body, at Sophia, don Rojas... and am slammed to the ground, the breath knocked from my lungs.

More gun shots. Machine gun fire. Yells and screams. The sound of a helicopter overhead. The hacienda is under attack!

Catching my breath, leaping to my feet, I run inside the hacienda and rush for the stairs, have to get my gun. A dead wolf lies in a puddle of spreading blood. It's disintegrating, becoming a cloud of particles. The housekeeper lays dead in the open doorway, she is changing into a cow, disintegrating. A man, one of don Rojas' workers/familiars staggers inside, bullet wounds in his chest, he falls to the ground, turns into a goat, dies, becomes a wisp of atoms and smoke.

I retrieve my colt 45, turn off the lights, sidle up to the bedroom window, peak outside. Jeeps, pickups, two Bell Huey helicopters on the ground. A UH-1B/C helicopter gunship in the air, with flood lights blazing and a soldier manning a M60 gatling machine gun looking for something to kill. On the ground, men and women in hoods. American soldiers with rifles and machine guns firing at wolves, lions, goats, rams, lions, cows, pigs, bids, creatures half-man half-beast. Creatures fall mortally wounded, turn to wisps of smoke, disappear.

I recognize the lieutenant. Snake Eyes!

"Mother fucker!"

And spreading out, at intervals, hooded men and women. I recognize Terranza's son, the priest, and from ULTRA, from the Institute, psychic warriors: witches, warlocks, psychics, and wizards. I understand instantly what's happening and why. The Company had learned from the clusterfuck in the highlands of Vietnam. It takes a sorcerer to catch a sorcerer.

The priest, the fucking priest led them here! And Snake Eyes, ULTRA, The Company, has supplied him with psychic weaponry. They joined forces!

Fuck me, I'm so stupid. I'd been warned. I should have gone back and killed that goddamned evil fucking priest.

I close the bedroom door. No light behind me. I open the bedroom window: the battle continues, the psychic warriors, the men and women beneath the hoods, they are spreading out. I can no longer see the priest or the Lt.

More gun shots. Machine gun fire. Blasts from the airborne helicopter.

I take aim, fire. A soldier with a machine gun goes down. I fire again. A soldier with a rifle collapses. The helicopter gun ship is directing its flood lights at the floor below me, the room next to mine. I take aim, fire, the soldier manning the helicopter machine gun falls, hangs dangling in the air, swinging from a bungee cord attached to the cabin door.

The soldiers on the ground direct their firepower at the upper story, at my window, blowing gaping holes in the walls. I have already thrown myself to the floor, and crawl toward the bedroom door.

I rush down the stairs. But the gun fire has stopped. All the defending half-man-half-animal servant/familiars must be dead.

An amplified voice over a loud speaker booms: "We have you surrounded. There is no escape. You cannot defeat us. We have weaponry you are powerless to resist. Weapons you cannot fight. We give you five minutes to step outside with hands up and surrender. You will not be harmed."

don Rojas, Sophia, are in a state of shock and awe. Windows blown out. Bullet holes in the walls. Priceless art and relics blown to hell. They don't understand what's happening, or why.

I quickly explain. "The priest, he's joined forced with your enemies. He must have cloaked himself and the others in darkness, which is what Owl Woman warned. That's why Sophia was unable to see him or the future."

don Rojas bravely approached the shattered double stained glass door and peered outside. "Those are American soldiers! And the others, what are they? Brujas? Led by the priest? Why are they here?" he asked.

"They've come for you, don Rojas," I said. "They intend to make you a prisoner, to help them with their experiments."

"What are these experiments?" don Rojas demanded.

"I'm not sure. A research institute in California. The U.S. military. Maybe the CIA."

Sophia, her face a mask of rage, slapped my face and screamed: "Evil follows you. You led them here! Bastardo! Bastardo! Nos traicionaste. ¡Traidor! Bastardo!"

"Sophia," I shout, grabbing hold of her hands. "No I didn't. I swear to you. It was the priest. I asked him how to find don Rojas. The soldiers must have asked him the same question."

"But you knew of this!" Sophia screamed at me.

don Rojas, standing at the shattered door, peering outside, spoke without turning around. "Sophia. daughter. He warned us of the priest. Our amigo did not betray us. He tells truth. It is the priest, el hijo de Terranza, who leads these enemies. I sense many brujas outside this door. Like the priest, they are weak. Together they are strong."

Sophia joined her father at the shattered double stained glass door. "Papa. I will see into their minds." She closed her eyes, hard in concentration, and said: "There are many crazy people. They have been trained by the Americans to become magicians of the mind."

Opening her eyes she turned and looked at me: "What is this: 'psychic warriors?'"

don Rojas interrupted: "We must kill the priest. Without the priest, the witches, and these psychic warriors lose mucho power."

I stepped forward; 'I can kill the priest. But there's over two dozen soldiers out there. Even if I had enough bullets I can't kill them all. The only solution is for you two to escape and get the hell out of here."

An amplified voice again boomed from outside: "You have two minutes. If you do not surrender, we will destroy this house and kill everyone inside."

don Rojas drew next to Sophia. They stood together talking quietly, Sophia nodding her head in agreement and understanding. Then she ran for the stairway.

don Rojas turned to me: "If you wish to help us. Please step outside. Tell them we will surrender."

"What? Why?" I exclaimed. "Can't you just change to birds or wolves, and get away?"

don Rojas put his hand on my shoulder. "No. They will follow. And, we cannot leave the hacienda, this ranchero, behind. Very dangerous. There is much magic here."

"But, if you surrender, the hacienda will still be here!" I argued.

"There is no time to explain. What we ask you to do, is very dangerous to your life. When the time comes, you must kill the priest then close your eyes."

"The priest? Gladly," I answered. "But why close my eyes?"

"Because you will be in great danger," don Rojas replied.

Sophia returned, holding four small satchels. "If you love me, do as my father asks," she said.

"Of course, I love you! With all my heart! But surrender. No! They'll put you both in a cage. Stick electrodes in your brain. You can't let them do that. There must be another way!"

don Rojas took two of the satchels from Sophia and said to me: "Do not worry, my Gringo Amigo. All we ask is for you to step outside, announce our surrender. Please kill the priest when, in your mind's eye, you hear me say, 'now.'"

"I can kill more than just the priest!" I exclaimed.

"The Priest will be enough," don Rojas answered. "And remember: We choose our own destiny. There is more than one future. We each have multiple futures. A true sorcerer can change his future and the past."

I turned to Sophia: "I'm so sorry. Honestly, Sophia, I never wanted this to happen. I, do love you. Care about you. More than you'd believe."

"I know. Now go," she replied.

I stepped outside, hands in the air, my Colt 45 stuck in the back of my pants

The Lt shouted: "Where's the sorcerer and the witch?"

"They've agreed to surrender," I answered. "Put down your guns. They're coming out."

A moment later, Sophia and don Rojas stepped outside, their faces glowing, arms and hands in the air, singing and chanting oaths, curses, and incantations. The soldiers did not lower their guns, but pointed them at our heads.

The psychic warriors, the priest and a dozen of his minions, stepped forward, forming a semi-circle, touching hands, mumbling devil-worshipping prayers.

With one hand, don Rojas, still singing, his face aglow with light, tossed the contents of a single satchel in the air forming a cloud of sparkling glittery star dust which drifted upwards. Simultaneously, Sophia, chanting incantations, her face aglow with light, tossed the contents of a second satchel in the air, forming a smoky cloud of black particles.

Dark clouds appeared and began obscuring the moon. There was a brilliant flash of lightning, and before the thunder could reach my ears, a voice in my mind cried: "Now."

Remembering the vision of my death, lying with bullets in my chest, I threw myself to the ground as I shot the priest through the head.

There was another flash of lightning, zig zagging, ripping across the sky and at the same moment Sophia and don Rojas each tossed fistfuls of tiny diamond-and-tiny-crescent-shaped-moons of sparkling light into the electrified air.

A huge thunder clap shook the earth. But I didn't close my eyes, intending instead to kill as many as I had bullets. Important to take out the leadership. I got the Lt next, winged him in the shoulder, slamming him to the ground.

A fierce wind struck, lighting streaked and flashed, explosions of thunder boomed. Sophia and don Rojas their bodies now radiating a bright aura of light, their hands reaching for the storming sky, continued to sing and chant. Thunder roared and there was another flash of lighting so blindingly bright the soldiers and I couldn't see at all.

And then, as I regained my sight, there were dozens of beautiful ghostly angelic beings flying in the electrified air, the stormy sky now illuminated by cloudy-ghostly waves of crimson and green. The soldiers, who like me, were just beginning to regain their sight, were not firing, but staring awe-struck at these divine creatures.

My eyes fell upon don Rojas and Sophia, their arms still upraised above their heads, their bodies radiating a glowing light--and from their hands lighting flashed, and around them angels flew as if they were being conjured out of the ghostly clouds of green and blue and emerging from thin air.

And then, the Lt, wounded but still alive, shattered that divine moment, yelling: "Fire. Kill them all!"

The angels became savage, hideously demonic, serpentine, lovely faces now shark-fanged snapping jaws, hands transformed into razor sharp ripping claws. Soldiers screamed, fired their guns, cried in nightmarish pain and fear, the angelic demons biting and clawing and tearing out livers, lungs, hearts, arms, legs and heads, and consuming the departing souls of the dead.

It was over in minutes, a blood soaked massacre of soldiers, witches, warlocks, and psychic warriors who'd suffered total defeat. don Rojas, Sophia , the demonic-angels, had killed them all!

The angelic demons, after sating their feast of souls, soared high and formed a flowing circle far overhead above the ranchero and hacienda. Nor was the storm over, for a strong wind howled and blew, thunder cracked and lightning ripped and zig zagged across the greenish-blue hued landscape and sky.

My eyes met those of Sophia, the woman who I dearly loved. But then, as I stood, intending to rush forward and take her in my arms, don Rojas held up a hand to stop me, and sadly shook his head "no." Taking Sophia by the hand, they turned, and as the whirlwind blew and the demonic-angels flew in circles high above, they walked back to the hacienda, their bodies still glowing, and closed the shattered door.

The angelic demons circled with a whirlwind fury, which grew to tornado strength above the ranchero and hacienda which began to creak and groan. Slowly the castle-like hacienda broke free of the earth with a terrific wrenching moan, and was lifted twisting, then spinning round and round into the air... I myself, was lifted from the ground by the hurricane winds that blew, but the hacienda flew even higher as it levitated and spun, spinning higher with the whirl of the wind, faster, growing smaller and smaller still, and then as lightning streaked across the green-blue sky, PUFF, the hacienda, ranchero, the storm, whirlwind, everything was gone, sucked into a tiny black hole, and disappearing into thin air.

Released from the hurricane winds I fell.

Stunned and shocked by this unexpected disappearing act, I could not tear my eyes from where the hacienda had been but was no more. I strode to and fro, in a daze, looking for a sign, any evidence; but even the foundation was gone. What had been fields of vegetables, corn, wheat, and fruit, were now nothing more than upturned dirt. There was no evidence, nothing left that would suggest a ranchero and hacienda had ever stood on this ground.

But this wasn't possible!

Slowly I turned my gaze upon the death, destruction, and wreckage left in its wake. Chunks of gore and flesh, severed arms, legs, heads, mangled bodies strewn about; jeeps, trucks, helicopters overturned, crushed and burnt.

I found what was left of the Lt. There was a fist-sized hole where his face should have been, another gaping hole on the left side of his chest. There were soldiers in worse shape, missing arms, legs, heads, and sporting a fist-size holes where their heart should have been. And of the scattered remains of the witches, warlocks, psychic warriors, their chest cavities had been ripped open, their broken bloody ribs protruding outward this way and that.

Of the priest nothing could be found. Nor was there any evidence of who or what killed them. No, not kill. This was a brutal slaughter, annihilation, a massacre.

I walked around, stunned, staggered, looking for some evidence of the animals, spirit-helpers, servants, but there was nothing.

Nothing. Nothing. Nothing. The animals, crops, don Rojas, Sophia, the hacienda, ranchero, all had vanished completely, as if they had never even existed.

I was alone. Abandoned.

I knew, in my heart, Sophia, don Rojas, they were gone forever.

I was shocked. Stunned.

I had lost, everything! Eden! The gates of paradise. Sophia!

I walked back and forth like a madman, tears in my eyes, dashed hopes and dreams and catastrophic loss overwhelming me. Sophia! Precious love lost. Never to hold her in my arms again... Never to become a sorcerer's apprentice...alien technologies lost to me... Never to see through the eyes of gods.... magic, access to alternate realities, Eden, the Gates of paradise, the knowledge of the gods... All lost to me forever.

Sophia, the love of my life, gone...

And it was all my fault!

My heart ached.

I had lost everything. I had failed all. Betrayed even myself. The dream was over. And it was all my fault.

What have I done! What have I done! I have lost, everything!

"Sophia! I LOVE YOU!" I yelled in anguish to the heavens. "And I am so sorry!"

Slumping to the ground, mentally exhausted, drained of energy, feeling totally defeated, I closed my eyes and sobbed and cried...whispering "Sophia" and remembering her lips against mine...

A fluttering breeze swirled through my hair. The sound of flapping wings teased my ears.

Opening my crying eyes I gazed through the dusty, fly-specked windshield of my VW. A black crow was standing on the hood of my car. It cocked its head to the left and right staring at me as I stared back.

I looked around. A short, fat sweating woman and two dirty, squirming brats stood in a dilapidated doorway. Two old men sat on a bench in the shade of a stack of tires. A tall thin Mexican man was striding toward my car, a dirty rag in his hands.

And then, the crow flapped its wings, and was gone.

Made in the USA
Monee, IL
09 September 2022

13666454R00083